www.Testinar.com

... So Much More Online!

✓ FREE Math lessons

✓ More Math learning books!

✓ Mathematics Worksheets

✓ Online Math Tutors

Need a PDF version of this book?

Please visit www.Testinar.com

AFOQT Math Practice Workbook 2020-2021

Abundant Skill-Building Math Exercises and 2 Full-Length AFOQT Math Practice Tests

By

Jay Daie & Reza Nazari

Copyright © 2020

Tesinar.com

All rights reserved. No part of this publication may be reproduced, stored in a retrieval system, or transmitted in any form or by any means, electronic, mechanical, photocopying, recording, scanning, or otherwise, except as permitted under Section 107 or 108 of the 1976 United States Copyright Ac, without permission of the author.

All inquiries should be addressed to:

info@Testinar.com

www.Testinar.com

ISBN: 978-1-64612-456-5

Published by: Testinar Inc

www.Testinar.com

Visit www.Testinar.com
for Online Math Practice

Description

AFOQT Math Practice Workbook 2020-2021, which reflects the 2020-2021 test guidelines, represents abundant Math exercises, sample AFOQT Math questions, and quizzes with answers and detailed solutions to help you hone your math skills, overcome your exam anxiety, boost your confidence—and do your best to succeed on the AFOQT Arithmetic Reasoning and Mathematics Knowledge tests. This is a precious math exercise book for AFOQT test-takers who need extra practice in math to ace the AFOQT Math test. Upon completion of this comprehensive math workbook, you will have a solid foundation and sufficient practice to defeat the AFOQT Math test. **This comprehensive practice book is your ticket to scoring higher on AFOQT Math.**

AFOQT Math Practice Workbook 2020-2021 with over 3,500 sample questions and over 8,000 online math questions will help you fully prepare for the AFOQT Arithmetic Reasoning and Mathematics Knowledge tests. Two full-length and realistic AFOQT Math practice tests with detailed answers and explanations that reflect the format and question types on the AFOQT are provided to check your exam-readiness and identify where you need more practice.

This comprehensive math workbook contains many exciting and unique features to help you improve your AFOQT Math test score, including:

- ✓ Content 100% aligned with the 2020 AFOQT test
- ✓ Complete coverage of all AFOQT Math concepts and topics which you will be tested
- ✓ Abundant Math skill-building exercises to help test-takers approach different question types that might be unfamiliar to them
- ✓ Over 8,000 additional AFOQT math online practice questions in both multiple-choice and grid-in formats with answers grouped by topic, so you can focus on your weak areas
- ✓ 2 full-length practice tests (featuring new question types) with detailed answers

This AFOQT Math practice workbook and other Testinar books are used by thousands of students each year to help them review core content areas, brush-up in math, discover their strengths and weaknesses, and achieve their best scores on the AFOQT test.

Contents

Whole Number Addition and Subtraction	3
Whole Number Multiplication and Division	5
Simplifying Fractions	7
Adding and Subtracting Fractions	9
Multiplying and Dividing Fractions	11
Adding Mixed Numbers	13
Subtract Mixed Numbers	15
Multiplying Mixed Numbers	17
Dividing Mixed Numbers	19
Comparing Decimals	21
Rounding Decimals	23
Multiplying and Dividing Decimals	25
Converting Between Fractions, Decimals and Mixed Numbers	27
Adding and Subtracting Integers	29
Multiplying and Dividing Integers	31
Order of Operation	33
Integers and Absolute Value	35
Writing Ratios	37
Simplifying Ratios	39
Similar Figures	41
Proportional Ratios	43
Percent Calculation	45
Converting Between Percent, Fractions, and Decimals	47
Percent Problems	49
Markup, Discount, and Tax	51
Simple Interest	53
Expressions and Variables	55
Simplifying Variable Expressions	57
Simplifying Polynomial Expressions	59
The Distributive Property	61
Evaluating One Variable	63
Evaluating Two Variables	65
Combining like Terms	67
One-Step Equations	69
Two-Step Equations	71
Multi-Step Equations	73
System of Equations	75
Systems of Equations Word Problems	77
Quadratic Equations	79
Graphing Single-Variable Inequalities	81

One-Step Inequalities	83
Two-Step Inequalities	85
Multi-Step Inequalities	87
Multiplication Property of Exponent	89
Division Property of Exponent	91
Powers of Products and Quotients	93
Zero and Negative Exponents	95
Negative Exponents and Negative Bases	97
Square Roots	99
Graphing Lines Using Slope-Intercept Form	101
Graphing Lines Using Standard Form	103
Writing Linear Equations	105
Graphing Linear Inequalities	107
Finding Slope	109
Finding Midpoint	111
Finding Distance of Two Points	113
Writing Polynomials in Standard Form	115
Simplifying Polynomials	117
Adding and Subtracting Polynomials	119
Multiplying Monomials	121
Multiplying Binomials	123
Factoring Trinomials	125
Dividing Monomials	127
Scientific Notation	129
Mean, Median, Mode, and Range of the Given Data	131
Pie Graph	133
Probability Problems	135
The Pythagorean Theorem	137
Angle and Area of Triangles	139
Perimeter of Polygons	141
Area and Circumference of Circles	143
Area of Squares, Rectangles, and Parallelograms	145
Area of Trapezoids	147
Angles	149
Volume of Cubes	151
Volume of Rectangle Prisms	153
Surface Area of Cubes	155
Surface Area of a Rectangle Prism	157
Volume of a Cylinder	159
Surface Area of a Cylinder	161
Function Notation	163

Adding and Subtracting Functions	165
Multiplying and Dividing Functions	167
Composition of Functions	169
AFOQT Test Review	171
AFOQT Mathematics Practice Tests	173
AFOQT Mathematics Practice Test 1	174
AFOQT Mathematics Practice Test 2	187
AFOQT Mathematics Practice Tests Answer Keys	199
AFOQT Mathematics Practice Tests Answers and Explanations	200

Whole Number Addition and Subtraction

✏️ **Find the missing number.**

1) $850 - \underline{} = 580$ 2) $770 + \underline{} = 1170$

3) $240 + \underline{} = 580$ 4) $940 + \underline{} = 1370$

5) $810 + \underline{} = 1420$ 6) $460 + \underline{} = 1350$

7) $560 + \underline{} = 1460$ 8) $470 + \underline{} = 940$

9) $890 + \underline{} = 1230$ 10) $960 - \underline{} = 210$

✏️ **Solve.**

1) $4,324 \\ -\underline{3,604}$ 2) $1,786 \\ +\underline{689}$ 3) $4,559 \\ -\underline{583}$

4) $3,337 \\ -\underline{3,127}$ 5) $3,816 \\ +\underline{940}$ 6) $3,760 \\ -\underline{3,286}$

7) $4,770 \\ -\underline{2,021}$ 8) $4,559 \\ +\underline{4,346}$ 9) $3,763 \\ +\underline{1,786}$

10) $4,876 \\ +\underline{564}$ 11) $4,465 \\ +\underline{1,749}$ 12) $3,666 \\ +\underline{1,378}$

Answers of Whole Number Addition and Subtraction

✏️ **Find the missing number.**

1) $850 - 270 = 580$

2) $770 + 400 = 1170$

3) $240 + 340 = 580$

4) $940 + 430 = 1370$

5) $810 + 610 = 1420$

6) $460 + 890 = 1350$

7) $560 + 900 = 1460$

8) $470 + 470 = 940$

9) $890 + 340 = 1230$

10) $960 - 750 = 210$

✏️ **Solve.**

1) $\begin{array}{r} 4,324 \\ -\ 3,604 \\ \hline 720 \end{array}$

2) $\begin{array}{r} 1,786 \\ +\ \ \ 689 \\ \hline 2,475 \end{array}$

3) $\begin{array}{r} 4,559 \\ -\ \ \ 583 \\ \hline 3,976 \end{array}$

4) $\begin{array}{r} 3,337 \\ -\ 3,127 \\ \hline 210 \end{array}$

5) $\begin{array}{r} 3,816 \\ +\ \ \ 940 \\ \hline 4,756 \end{array}$

6) $\begin{array}{r} 3,760 \\ -\ 3,286 \\ \hline 474 \end{array}$

7) $\begin{array}{r} 4,770 \\ -\ 2,021 \\ \hline 2,749 \end{array}$

8) $\begin{array}{r} 4,559 \\ +\ 4,346 \\ \hline 8,905 \end{array}$

9) $\begin{array}{r} 3,763 \\ +\ 1,786 \\ \hline 5,549 \end{array}$

10) $\begin{array}{r} 4,876 \\ +\ \ \ 564 \\ \hline 5,440 \end{array}$

11) $\begin{array}{r} 4,465 \\ +\ 1,749 \\ \hline 6,214 \end{array}$

12) $\begin{array}{r} 3,666 \\ +\ 1,378 \\ \hline 5,044 \end{array}$

Whole Number Multiplication and Division

✏️ Calculate.

1) 828 ÷ 36 =

2) 10 × 10 =

3) 350 ÷ 25 =

4) 3780 ÷ 84 =

5) 46 × 32 =

6) 28028 ÷ 98 =

7) 4402 ÷ 71 =

8) 20856 ÷ 24 =

9) 7854 ÷ 51 =

10) 1012 × 60 =

11) 10153 ÷ 71 =

12) 1952 ÷ 32 =

13) 697 ÷ 41 =

14) 330 × 48 =

15) 58 × 52 =

16) 1152 ÷ 24 =

17) 910 ÷ 14 =

18) 473 × 24 =

19) 1078 × 15 =

20) 352 × 75 =

21) 44 × 38 =

22) 95 × 77 =

23) 8099 ÷ 91 =

24) 2945 ÷ 31 =

25) 22264 ÷ 44 =

26) 20460 ÷ 60 =

27) 902 × 22 =

28) 363 × 64 =

29) 38775 ÷ 75 =

30) 90 × 31 =

Answers of Whole Number Multiplication and Division

✏️ **Calculate.**

1) $828 \div 36 = 23$
2) $10 \times 10 = 100$
3) $350 \div 25 = 14$

4) $3780 \div 84 = 45$
5) $46 \times 32 = 1472$
6) $28028 \div 98 = 286$

7) $4402 \div 71 = 62$
8) $20856 \div 24 = 869$
9) $7854 \div 51 = 154$

10) $1012 \times 60 = 60720$
11) $10153 \div 71 = 143$
12) $1952 \div 32 = 61$

13) $697 \div 41 = 17$
14) $330 \times 48 = 15840$
15) $58 \times 52 = 3016$

16) $1152 \div 24 = 48$
17) $910 \div 14 = 65$
18) $473 \times 24 = 11352$

19) $1078 \times 15 = 16170$
20) $352 \times 75 = 26400$
21) $44 \times 38 = 1672$

22) $95 \times 77 = 7315$
23) $8099 \div 91 = 89$
24) $2945 \div 31 = 95$

25) $22264 \div 44 = 506$
26) $20460 \div 60 = 341$
27) $902 \times 22 = 19844$

28) $363 \times 64 = 23232$
29) $38775 \div 75 = 517$
30) $90 \times 31 = 2790$

Simplifying Fractions

✏️ **Simplify the fractions.**

1) $\frac{80}{95} =$

2) $\frac{70}{105} =$

3) $\frac{9}{12} =$

4) $\frac{45}{48} =$

5) $\frac{70}{85} =$

6) $\frac{30}{51} =$

7) $\frac{39}{60} =$

8) $\frac{50}{85} =$

9) $\frac{39}{48} =$

10) $\frac{42}{63} =$

11) $\frac{15}{30} =$

12) $\frac{75}{110} =$

13) $\frac{95}{110} =$

14) $\frac{55}{70} =$

15) $\frac{48}{69} =$

16) $\frac{15}{18} =$

17) $\frac{25}{40} =$

18) $\frac{50}{65} =$

19) $\frac{85}{120} =$

20) $\frac{30}{33} =$

21) $\frac{12}{21} =$

22) $\frac{45}{60} =$

23) $\frac{45}{66} =$

24) $\frac{40}{75} =$

25) $\frac{57}{78} =$

26) $\frac{18}{39} =$

27) $\frac{27}{36} =$

28) $\frac{60}{75} =$

29) $\frac{90}{125} =$

30) $\frac{45}{54} =$

31) $\frac{100}{135} =$

32) $\frac{30}{39} =$

33) $\frac{36}{57} =$

Answers of Simplifying Fractions

✏️ **Simplify the fractions.**

1) $\dfrac{80}{95} = \dfrac{16}{19}$ 2) $\dfrac{70}{105} = \dfrac{14}{21}$ 3) $\dfrac{9}{12} = \dfrac{3}{4}$

4) $\dfrac{45}{48} = \dfrac{15}{16}$ 5) $\dfrac{70}{85} = \dfrac{14}{17}$ 6) $\dfrac{30}{51} = \dfrac{10}{17}$

7) $\dfrac{39}{60} = \dfrac{13}{20}$ 8) $\dfrac{50}{85} = \dfrac{10}{17}$ 9) $\dfrac{39}{48} = \dfrac{13}{16}$

10) $\dfrac{42}{63} = \dfrac{14}{21}$ 11) $\dfrac{15}{30} = \dfrac{3}{6}$ 12) $\dfrac{75}{110} = \dfrac{15}{22}$

13) $\dfrac{95}{110} = \dfrac{19}{22}$ 14) $\dfrac{55}{70} = \dfrac{11}{14}$ 15) $\dfrac{48}{69} = \dfrac{16}{23}$

16) $\dfrac{15}{18} = \dfrac{5}{6}$ 17) $\dfrac{25}{40} = \dfrac{5}{8}$ 18) $\dfrac{50}{65} = \dfrac{10}{13}$

19) $\dfrac{85}{120} = \dfrac{17}{24}$ 20) $\dfrac{30}{33} = \dfrac{10}{11}$ 21) $\dfrac{12}{21} = \dfrac{4}{7}$

22) $\dfrac{45}{60} = \dfrac{9}{12}$ 23) $\dfrac{45}{66} = \dfrac{15}{22}$ 24) $\dfrac{40}{75} = \dfrac{8}{15}$

25) $\dfrac{57}{78} = \dfrac{19}{26}$ 26) $\dfrac{18}{39} = \dfrac{6}{13}$ 27) $\dfrac{27}{36} = \dfrac{9}{12}$

28) $\dfrac{60}{75} = \dfrac{12}{15}$ 29) $\dfrac{90}{125} = \dfrac{18}{25}$ 30) $\dfrac{45}{54} = \dfrac{15}{18}$

31) $\dfrac{100}{135} = \dfrac{20}{27}$ 32) $\dfrac{30}{39} = \dfrac{10}{13}$ 33) $\dfrac{36}{57} = \dfrac{12}{19}$

Adding and Subtracting Fractions

Solve.

1) $\frac{9}{9} + \frac{7}{2} =$ 2) $\frac{7}{9} + \frac{7}{3} =$ 3) $\frac{6}{6} + \frac{6}{2} =$

4) $\frac{15}{9} + \frac{11}{11} =$ 5) $\frac{11}{9} + \frac{11}{10} =$ 6) $\frac{13}{14} + \frac{15}{15} =$

7) $\frac{14}{9} + \frac{13}{14} =$ 8) $\frac{8}{8} + \frac{11}{12} =$ 9) $\frac{9}{8} + \frac{8}{2} =$

10) $\frac{13}{12} + \frac{18}{11} =$ 11) $\frac{12}{8} + \frac{12}{13} =$ 12) $\frac{9}{4} + \frac{8}{4} =$

13) $\frac{8}{7} + \frac{4}{4} =$ 14) $\frac{10}{12} + \frac{16}{17} =$ 15) $\frac{14}{15} + \frac{18}{10} =$

Solve.

1) $\frac{8}{6} - \frac{1}{3} =$ 2) $\frac{8}{5} - \frac{1}{8} =$ 3) $\frac{17}{7} - \frac{17}{16} =$

4) $\frac{15}{11} - \frac{18}{16} =$ 5) $\frac{18}{10} - \frac{16}{17} =$ 6) $\frac{7}{4} - \frac{6}{5} =$

7) $\frac{6}{3} - \frac{4}{4} =$ 8) $\frac{6}{8} - \frac{2}{3} =$ 9) $\frac{15}{12} - \frac{11}{12} =$

10) $\frac{17}{5} - \frac{14}{13} =$ 11) $\frac{6}{3} - \frac{5}{5} =$ 12) $\frac{8}{3} - \frac{6}{4} =$

13) $\frac{5}{2} - \frac{3}{2} =$ 14) $\frac{21}{2} - \frac{15}{18} =$ 15) $\frac{24}{3} - \frac{12}{18} =$

16) $\frac{7}{5} - \frac{7}{7} =$ 17) $\frac{5}{4} - \frac{3}{6} =$ 18) $\frac{24}{4} - \frac{17}{14} =$

Answers of Adding and Subtracting Fractions

Solve.

1) $\frac{9}{9} + \frac{7}{2} = \frac{9}{2}$
2) $\frac{7}{9} + \frac{7}{3} = \frac{28}{9}$
3) $\frac{6}{6} + \frac{6}{2} = \frac{4}{1}$

4) $\frac{15}{9} + \frac{11}{11} = \frac{8}{3}$
5) $\frac{11}{9} + \frac{11}{10} = \frac{209}{90}$
6) $\frac{13}{14} + \frac{15}{15} = \frac{27}{14}$

7) $\frac{14}{9} + \frac{13}{14} = \frac{313}{126}$
8) $\frac{8}{8} + \frac{11}{12} = \frac{23}{12}$
9) $\frac{9}{8} + \frac{8}{2} = \frac{41}{8}$

10) $\frac{13}{12} + \frac{18}{11} = \frac{359}{132}$
11) $\frac{12}{8} + \frac{12}{13} = \frac{63}{26}$
12) $\frac{9}{4} + \frac{8}{4} = \frac{17}{4}$

13) $\frac{8}{7} + \frac{4}{4} = \frac{15}{7}$
14) $\frac{10}{12} + \frac{16}{17} = \frac{181}{102}$
15) $\frac{14}{15} + \frac{18}{10} = \frac{41}{15}$

Solve.

1) $\frac{8}{6} - \frac{1}{3} = \frac{1}{1}$
2) $\frac{8}{5} - \frac{1}{8} = \frac{59}{40}$
3) $\frac{17}{7} - \frac{17}{16} = \frac{153}{112}$

4) $\frac{15}{11} - \frac{18}{16} = \frac{21}{88}$
5) $\frac{18}{10} - \frac{16}{17} = \frac{73}{85}$
6) $\frac{7}{4} - \frac{6}{5} = \frac{11}{20}$

7) $\frac{6}{3} - \frac{4}{4} = \frac{1}{1}$
8) $\frac{6}{8} - \frac{2}{3} = \frac{1}{12}$
9) $\frac{15}{12} - \frac{11}{12} = \frac{1}{3}$

10) $\frac{17}{5} - \frac{14}{13} = \frac{151}{65}$
11) $\frac{6}{3} - \frac{5}{5} = \frac{1}{1}$
12) $\frac{8}{3} - \frac{6}{4} = \frac{7}{6}$

13) $\frac{5}{2} - \frac{3}{2} = \frac{1}{1}$
14) $\frac{21}{2} - \frac{15}{18} = \frac{29}{3}$
15) $\frac{24}{3} - \frac{12}{18} = \frac{22}{3}$

16) $\frac{7}{5} - \frac{7}{7} = \frac{2}{5}$
17) $\frac{5}{4} - \frac{3}{6} = \frac{3}{4}$
18) $\frac{24}{4} - \frac{17}{14} = \frac{67}{14}$

Multiplying and Dividing Fractions

✏️ **Multiply the fractions and simplify if needed.**

1) $\frac{9}{9} \times \frac{11}{15} = \frac{99}{135}$

2) $\frac{3}{5} \times \frac{13}{15} = \frac{13}{25}$

3) $\frac{5}{3} \times \frac{13}{11} =$

4) $\frac{9}{7} \times \frac{6}{5} =$

5) $\frac{6}{10} \times \frac{4}{7} =$

6) $\frac{9}{7} \times \frac{15}{18} =$

7) $\frac{4}{5} \times \frac{6}{4} = \frac{6}{5}$

8) $\frac{2}{2} \times \frac{8}{4} =$

9) $\frac{4}{6} \times \frac{18}{17} =$

10) $\frac{5}{3} \times \frac{5}{4} =$

11) $\frac{8}{10} \times \frac{7}{1} =$

12) $\frac{8}{2} \times \frac{17}{13} =$

13) $\frac{2}{3} \times \frac{4}{1} =$

14) $\frac{3}{4} \times \frac{11}{12} =$

15) $\frac{8}{6} \times \frac{15}{17} =$

✏️ **Dividing fractions. Then simplify.**

1) $\frac{8}{8} \div \frac{7}{2} = \frac{2}{7} \quad \frac{16}{56} = \frac{2}{7}$

2) $\frac{6}{9} \div \frac{8}{4} \quad \frac{4}{8} \quad \frac{24}{72} = \frac{1}{3}$

3) $\frac{6}{4} \div \frac{7}{6} \quad \frac{6}{7} \quad \frac{36}{28} = \frac{9}{7}$

4) $\frac{5}{4} \div \frac{3}{6} =$

5) $\frac{7}{9} \div \frac{1}{8} =$

6) $\frac{8}{2} \div \frac{5}{5} =$

7) $\frac{9}{8} \div \frac{5}{4} =$

8) $\frac{8}{4} \div \frac{8}{7} =$

9) $\frac{7}{4} \div \frac{3}{1} =$

10) $\frac{9}{5} \div \frac{2}{3} =$

11) $\frac{3}{4} \div \frac{2}{1} =$

12) $\frac{3}{3} \div \frac{3}{3} =$

13) $\frac{8}{6} \div \frac{6}{7} =$

14) $\frac{2}{5} \div \frac{1}{7} =$

15) $\frac{6}{7} \div \frac{5}{6} =$

16) $\frac{2}{2} \div \frac{8}{1} =$

17) $\frac{3}{5} \div \frac{6}{3} =$

18) $\frac{8}{10} \div \frac{8}{3} =$

Answers of Multiplying and Dividing Fractions

Multiply the fractions and simplify if needed.

1) $\frac{9}{9} \times \frac{11}{15} = \frac{11}{15}$ 2) $\frac{3}{5} \times \frac{13}{15} = \frac{13}{25}$ 3) $\frac{5}{3} \times \frac{13}{11} = \frac{65}{33}$

4) $\frac{9}{7} \times \frac{6}{5} = \frac{54}{35}$ 5) $\frac{6}{10} \times \frac{4}{7} = \frac{12}{35}$ 6) $\frac{9}{7} \times \frac{15}{18} = \frac{15}{14}$

7) $\frac{4}{5} \times \frac{6}{4} = \frac{6}{5}$ 8) $\frac{2}{2} \times \frac{8}{4} = \frac{2}{1}$ 9) $\frac{4}{6} \times \frac{18}{17} = \frac{12}{17}$

10) $\frac{5}{3} \times \frac{5}{4} = \frac{25}{12}$ 11) $\frac{8}{10} \times \frac{7}{1} = \frac{28}{5}$ 12) $\frac{8}{2} \times \frac{17}{13} = \frac{68}{13}$

13) $\frac{2}{3} \times \frac{4}{1} = \frac{8}{3}$ 14) $\frac{3}{4} \times \frac{11}{12} = \frac{11}{16}$ 15) $\frac{8}{6} \times \frac{15}{17} = \frac{20}{17}$

Dividing fractions. Then simplify.

1) $\frac{8}{8} \div \frac{7}{2} = \frac{2}{7}$ 2) $\frac{6}{9} \div \frac{8}{4} = \frac{1}{3}$ 3) $\frac{6}{4} \div \frac{7}{6} = \frac{9}{7}$

4) $\frac{5}{4} \div \frac{3}{6} = \frac{5}{2}$ 5) $\frac{7}{9} \div \frac{1}{8} = \frac{56}{9}$ 6) $\frac{8}{2} \div \frac{5}{5} = \frac{4}{1}$

7) $\frac{9}{8} \div \frac{5}{4} = \frac{9}{10}$ 8) $\frac{8}{4} \div \frac{8}{7} = \frac{7}{4}$ 9) $\frac{7}{4} \div \frac{3}{1} = \frac{7}{12}$

10) $\frac{9}{5} \div \frac{2}{3} = \frac{27}{10}$ 11) $\frac{3}{4} \div \frac{2}{1} = \frac{3}{8}$ 12) $\frac{3}{3} \div \frac{3}{3} = \frac{1}{1} = 1$

13) $\frac{8}{6} \div \frac{6}{7} = \frac{14}{9}$ 14) $\frac{2}{5} \div \frac{1}{7} = \frac{14}{5}$ 15) $\frac{6}{7} \div \frac{5}{6} = \frac{36}{35}$

16) $\frac{2}{2} \div \frac{8}{1} = \frac{1}{8}$ 17) $\frac{3}{5} \div \frac{6}{3} = \frac{3}{10}$ 18) $\frac{8}{10} \div \frac{8}{3} = \frac{3}{10}$

Adding Mixed Numbers

Solve.

1) $4\frac{6}{2} + 7\frac{2}{4} =$

2) $4\frac{2}{2} + 5\frac{5}{2} =$

3) $4\frac{8}{10} + 3\frac{7}{1} =$

4) $2\frac{5}{2} + 4\frac{7}{3} =$

5) $4\frac{5}{10} + 2\frac{4}{4} =$

6) $7\frac{7}{10} + 1\frac{7}{1} =$

7) $6\frac{9}{8} + 2\frac{2}{1} =$

8) $2\frac{3}{5} + 6\frac{6}{1} =$

9) $1\frac{8}{8} + 1\frac{4}{7} =$

10) $6\frac{3}{10} + 8\frac{6}{5} =$

11) $3\frac{6}{5} + 3\frac{4}{1} =$

12) $4\frac{4}{2} + 7\frac{1}{3} =$

13) $8\frac{9}{2} + 3\frac{7}{1} =$

14) $6\frac{9}{6} + 5\frac{2}{6} =$

15) $2\frac{10}{7} + 1\frac{2}{4} =$

16) $5\frac{9}{9} + 1\frac{3}{8} =$

17) $1\frac{3}{6} + 5\frac{5}{2} =$

18) $2\frac{10}{6} + 4\frac{3}{7} =$

19) $1\frac{5}{3} + 7\frac{2}{6} =$

20) $2\frac{7}{5} + 5\frac{1}{6} =$

21) $2\frac{5}{4} + 5\frac{4}{1} =$

22) $2\frac{9}{3} + 6\frac{2}{2} =$

Answers of Adding Mixed Numbers

Solve.

1) $4\frac{6}{2} + 7\frac{2}{4} = = 14\frac{1}{2}$

2) $4\frac{2}{2} + 5\frac{5}{2} = = 12\frac{1}{2}$

3) $4\frac{8}{10} + 3\frac{7}{1} = = 14\frac{4}{5}$

4) $2\frac{5}{2} + 4\frac{7}{3} = = 10\frac{5}{6}$

5) $4\frac{5}{10} + 2\frac{4}{4} = = 7\frac{1}{2}$

6) $7\frac{7}{10} + 1\frac{7}{1} = = 15\frac{7}{10}$

7) $6\frac{9}{8} + 2\frac{2}{1} = = 11\frac{1}{8}$

8) $2\frac{3}{5} + 6\frac{6}{1} = = 14\frac{3}{5}$

9) $1\frac{8}{8} + 1\frac{4}{7} = = 3\frac{4}{7}$

10) $6\frac{3}{10} + 8\frac{6}{5} = = 15\frac{1}{2}$

11) $3\frac{6}{5} + 3\frac{4}{1} = = 11\frac{1}{5}$

12) $4\frac{4}{2} + 7\frac{1}{3} = = 13\frac{1}{3}$

13) $8\frac{9}{2} + 3\frac{7}{1} = = 22\frac{1}{2}$

14) $6\frac{9}{6} + 5\frac{2}{6} = = 12\frac{5}{6}$

15) $2\frac{10}{7} + 1\frac{2}{4} = = 4\frac{13}{14}$

16) $5\frac{9}{9} + 1\frac{3}{8} = = 7\frac{3}{8}$

17) $1\frac{3}{6} + 5\frac{5}{2} = = 9\frac{0}{1}$

18) $2\frac{10}{6} + 4\frac{3}{7} = = 8\frac{2}{21}$

19) $1\frac{5}{3} + 7\frac{2}{6} = = 10\frac{0}{1}$

20) $2\frac{7}{5} + 5\frac{1}{6} = = 8\frac{17}{30}$

21) $2\frac{5}{4} + 5\frac{4}{1} = = 12\frac{1}{4}$

22) $2\frac{9}{3} + 6\frac{2}{2} = = 12\frac{0}{1}$

Subtract Mixed Numbers

✏️ Solve.

1) $7\frac{1}{1} - 4\frac{5}{6} =$

2) $4\frac{6}{3} - 2\frac{2}{7} =$

3) $3\frac{8}{8} - 1\frac{4}{9} =$

4) $7\frac{7}{6} - 5\frac{3}{7} =$

5) $6\frac{5}{8} - 1\frac{3}{5} =$

6) $6\frac{4}{2} - 1\frac{2}{4} =$

7) $8\frac{5}{6} - 5\frac{1}{4} =$

8) $5\frac{6}{4} - 2\frac{5}{5} =$

9) $5\frac{6}{7} - 2\frac{2}{8} =$

10) $6\frac{4}{4} - 1\frac{4}{7} =$

11) $5\frac{6}{1} - 4\frac{5}{3} =$

12) $10\frac{2}{1} - 4\frac{5}{4} =$

13) $6\frac{7}{7} - 2\frac{4}{5} =$

14) $5\frac{3}{1} - 1\frac{1}{2} =$

15) $8\frac{9}{5} - 6\frac{3}{2} =$

16) $5\frac{7}{6} - 2\frac{2}{5} =$

17) $4\frac{6}{10} - 1\frac{1}{10} =$

18) $10\frac{9}{1} - 2\frac{5}{8} =$

19) $8\frac{5}{1} - 1\frac{6}{6} =$

20) $6\frac{6}{1} - 5\frac{2}{4} =$

21) $5\frac{1}{1} - 2\frac{1}{7} =$

22) $7\frac{2}{7} - 1\frac{2}{8} =$

Answers of Subtract Mixed Numbers

Solve.

1) $7\frac{1}{1} - 4\frac{5}{6} = 3\frac{1}{6}$

2) $4\frac{6}{3} - 2\frac{2}{7} = 3\frac{5}{7}$

3) $3\frac{8}{8} - 1\frac{4}{9} = 2\frac{5}{9}$

4) $7\frac{7}{6} - 5\frac{3}{7} = 2\frac{31}{42}$

5) $6\frac{5}{8} - 1\frac{3}{5} = 5\frac{1}{40}$

6) $6\frac{4}{2} - 1\frac{2}{4} = 6\frac{1}{2}$

7) $8\frac{5}{6} - 5\frac{1}{4} = 3\frac{7}{12}$

8) $5\frac{6}{4} - 2\frac{5}{5} = 3\frac{1}{2}$

9) $5\frac{6}{7} - 2\frac{2}{8} = 3\frac{17}{28}$

10) $6\frac{4}{4} - 1\frac{4}{7} = 5\frac{3}{7}$

11) $5\frac{6}{1} - 4\frac{5}{3} = 5\frac{1}{3}$

12) $10\frac{2}{1} - 4\frac{5}{4} = 6\frac{3}{4}$

13) $6\frac{7}{7} - 2\frac{4}{5} = 4\frac{1}{5}$

14) $5\frac{3}{1} - 1\frac{1}{2} = 6\frac{1}{2}$

15) $8\frac{9}{5} - 6\frac{3}{2} = 2\frac{3}{10}$

16) $5\frac{7}{6} - 2\frac{2}{5} = 3\frac{23}{30}$

17) $4\frac{6}{10} - 1\frac{1}{10} = 3\frac{1}{2}$

18) $10\frac{9}{1} - 2\frac{5}{8} = 16\frac{3}{8}$

19) $8\frac{5}{1} - 1\frac{6}{6} = 11\frac{0}{1}$

20) $6\frac{6}{1} - 5\frac{2}{4} = 6\frac{1}{2}$

21) $5\frac{1}{1} - 2\frac{1}{7} = 3\frac{6}{7}$

22) $7\frac{2}{7} - 1\frac{2}{8} = 6\frac{1}{28}$

Multiplying Mixed Numbers

✏️ **Calculate.**

1) $4\frac{2}{3} \times 3\frac{3}{9} =$

2) $6\frac{4}{5} \times 4\frac{1}{9} =$

3) $6\frac{6}{9} \times 4\frac{2}{9} =$

4) $2\frac{7}{1} \times 1\frac{4}{9} =$

5) $10\frac{3}{4} \times 8\frac{6}{10} =$

6) $4\frac{7}{3} \times 2\frac{4}{10} =$

7) $6\frac{7}{2} \times 3\frac{4}{6} =$

8) $8\frac{5}{1} \times 1\frac{6}{3} =$

9) $6\frac{5}{1} \times 3\frac{2}{6} =$

10) $6\frac{7}{9} \times 2\frac{2}{6} =$

11) $7\frac{7}{8} \times 2\frac{3}{5} =$

12) $5\frac{2}{1} \times 4\frac{5}{3} =$

13) $3\frac{3}{1} \times 1\frac{7}{4} =$

14) $5\frac{6}{3} \times 4\frac{9}{5} =$

15) $4\frac{4}{3} \times 1\frac{6}{9} =$

16) $8\frac{5}{4} \times 2\frac{5}{8} =$

17) $7\frac{7}{5} \times 3\frac{1}{5} =$

18) $3\frac{6}{3} \times 1\frac{1}{3} =$

19) $2\frac{6}{4} \times 1\frac{3}{7} =$

20) $5\frac{9}{4} \times 4\frac{1}{2} =$

21) $8\frac{4}{1} \times 2\frac{1}{6} =$

22) $8\frac{4}{2} \times 4\frac{2}{5} =$

Answers of Multiplying Mixed Numbers

Calculate.

1) $4\frac{2}{3} \times 3\frac{3}{9} = 15\frac{5}{9}$

2) $6\frac{4}{5} \times 4\frac{1}{9} = 27\frac{43}{45}$

3) $6\frac{6}{9} \times 4\frac{2}{9} = 28\frac{4}{27}$

4) $2\frac{7}{1} \times 1\frac{4}{9} = 13$

5) $10\frac{3}{4} \times 8\frac{6}{10} = 92\frac{9}{20}$

6) $4\frac{7}{3} \times 2\frac{4}{10} = 15\frac{1}{5}$

7) $6\frac{7}{2} \times 3\frac{4}{6} = 34\frac{5}{6}$

8) $8\frac{5}{1} \times 1\frac{6}{3} = 39$

9) $6\frac{5}{1} \times 3\frac{2}{6} = 36\frac{2}{3}$

10) $6\frac{7}{9} \times 2\frac{2}{6} = 15\frac{22}{27}$

11) $7\frac{7}{8} \times 2\frac{3}{5} = 20\frac{19}{40}$

12) $5\frac{2}{1} \times 4\frac{5}{3} = 39\frac{2}{3}$

13) $3\frac{3}{1} \times 1\frac{7}{4} = 16\frac{1}{2}$

14) $5\frac{6}{3} \times 4\frac{9}{5} = 40\frac{3}{5}$

15) $4\frac{4}{3} \times 1\frac{6}{9} = 8\frac{8}{9}$

16) $8\frac{5}{4} \times 2\frac{5}{8} = 24\frac{9}{32}$

17) $7\frac{7}{5} \times 3\frac{1}{5} = 26\frac{22}{25}$

18) $3\frac{6}{3} \times 1\frac{1}{3} = 6\frac{2}{3}$

19) $2\frac{6}{4} \times 1\frac{3}{7} = 5$

20) $5\frac{9}{4} \times 4\frac{1}{2} = 32\frac{5}{8}$

21) $8\frac{4}{1} \times 2\frac{1}{6} = 26$

22) $8\frac{4}{2} \times 4\frac{2}{5} = 44$

Dividing Mixed Numbers

✏️ Solve.

1) $5\frac{5}{3} \div 2\frac{8}{7} =$

2) $8\frac{1}{5} \div 6\frac{1}{6} =$

3) $10\frac{4}{2} \div 3\frac{5}{10} =$

4) $5\frac{8}{4} \div 2\frac{5}{9} =$

5) $6\frac{3}{2} \div 1\frac{1}{3} =$

6) $7\frac{2}{9} \div 3\frac{1}{5} =$

7) $8\frac{9}{10} \div 4\frac{4}{5} =$

8) $7\frac{4}{5} \div 3\frac{1}{4} =$

9) $6\frac{6}{3} \div 1\frac{7}{6} =$

10) $6\frac{2}{1} \div 5\frac{4}{9} =$

11) $8\frac{4}{5} \div 2\frac{3}{5} =$

12) $7\frac{7}{2} \div 4\frac{3}{1} =$

13) $8\frac{8}{5} \div 1\frac{5}{7} =$

14) $8\frac{4}{6} \div 6\frac{2}{6} =$

15) $8\frac{9}{5} \div 3\frac{2}{7} =$

16) $10\frac{2}{5} \div 5\frac{2}{10} =$

17) $8\frac{9}{4} \div 1\frac{1}{3} =$

18) $7\frac{7}{4} \div 6\frac{6}{9} =$

19) $8\frac{2}{4} \div 1\frac{1}{9} =$

20) $8\frac{4}{3} \div 5\frac{3}{7} =$

21) $8\frac{7}{2} \div 6\frac{6}{5} =$

22) $8\frac{7}{2} \div 7\frac{6}{4} =$

Answers of Dividing Mixed Numbers

✏️ **Solve.**

1) $5\frac{5}{3} \div 2\frac{8}{7} = 2\frac{4}{33}$

2) $8\frac{1}{5} \div 6\frac{1}{6} = 1\frac{61}{185}$

3) $10\frac{4}{2} \div 3\frac{5}{10} = 3\frac{3}{7}$

4) $5\frac{8}{4} \div 2\frac{5}{9} = 2\frac{17}{23}$

5) $6\frac{3}{2} \div 1\frac{1}{3} = 5\frac{5}{8}$

6) $7\frac{2}{9} \div 3\frac{1}{5} = 2\frac{37}{144}$

7) $8\frac{9}{10} \div 4\frac{4}{5} = 1\frac{41}{48}$

8) $7\frac{4}{5} \div 3\frac{1}{4} = 2\frac{2}{5}$

9) $6\frac{6}{3} \div 1\frac{7}{6} = 3\frac{9}{13}$

10) $6\frac{2}{1} \div 5\frac{4}{9} = 1\frac{23}{49}$

11) $8\frac{4}{5} \div 2\frac{3}{5} = 3\frac{5}{13}$

12) $7\frac{7}{2} \div 4\frac{3}{1} = 1\frac{1}{2}$

13) $8\frac{8}{5} \div 1\frac{5}{7} = 5\frac{3}{5}$

14) $8\frac{4}{6} \div 6\frac{2}{6} = 1\frac{7}{19}$

15) $8\frac{9}{5} \div 3\frac{2}{7} = 2\frac{113}{115}$

16) $10\frac{2}{5} \div 5\frac{2}{10} = 2$

17) $8\frac{9}{4} \div 1\frac{1}{3} = 7\frac{11}{16}$

18) $7\frac{7}{4} \div 6\frac{6}{9} = 1\frac{5}{16}$

19) $8\frac{2}{4} \div 1\frac{1}{9} = 7\frac{13}{20}$

20) $8\frac{4}{3} \div 5\frac{3}{7} = 1\frac{41}{57}$

21) $8\frac{7}{2} \div 6\frac{6}{5} = 1\frac{43}{72}$

22) $8\frac{7}{2} \div 7\frac{6}{4} = 1\frac{6}{17}$

Comparing Decimals

✎ Use > = <.

1) 22.09 ☐ 94.88

2) 13.35 ☐ 67.76

3) 66.94 ☐ 66.94

4) 25.19 ☐ 22.71

5) 96.27 ☐ 96.27

6) 67.83 ☐ 19.93

7) 29.16 ☐ 0.43

8) 379.2 ☐ 37.92

9) 815.7 ☐ 81.57

10) 3.12 ☐ 3.12

11) 513.5 ☐ 51.35

12) 819.7 ☐ 81.97

13) 277.5 ☐ 27.75

14) 65.5 ☐ 42.81

15) 79.06 ☐ 39.16

16) 61.72 ☐ 6.172

17) 438.1 ☐ 43.81

18) 40.25 ☐ 40.25

19) 101.37 ☐ 93.83

20) 94.42 ☐ 34.66

21) 18.8 ☐ 1.88

22) 23.24 ☐ 96.95

Answers of Comparing Decimals

✏️ Use > = <.

1) 22.09 < 94.88
2) 13.35 < 67.76
3) 66.94 = 66.94
4) 25.19 > 22.71
5) 96.27 = 96.27
6) 67.83 > 19.93
7) 29.16 > 0.43
8) 379.2 > 37.92
9) 815.7 > 81.57
10) 3.12 = 3.12
11) 513.5 > 51.35
12) 819.7 > 81.97
13) 277.5 > 27.75
14) 65.5 > 42.81
15) 79.06 > 39.16
16) 61.72 > 6.172
17) 438.1 > 43.81
18) 40.25 = 40.25
19) 101.37 > 93.83
20) 94.42 > 34.66
21) 18.8 > 1.88
22) 23.24 < 96.95

Rounding Decimals

Round each decimal number to the nearest place indicated.

1) 16.2̲43   2) 10.28̲5   3) 10̲.590

4) 14.6̲43   5) 15̲.637   6) 15.9̲11

7) 17.33̲1   8) 13.67̲6   9) 13̲.496

Round each decimal to the nearest whole number.

1) 5.351   2) 21.188   3) 23.633

4) 26.586   5) 31.491   6) 11.106

7) 19.209   8) 29.205   9) 8.601

Round each decimal to the nearest tenth.

1) 68.347   2) 41.266   3) 45.782

4) 55.532   5) 65.674   6) 61.333

7) 63.801   8) 64.394   9) 49.501

Round each decimal to the nearest hundredth.

1) 51.392   2) 63.708   3) 64.951

4) 66.152   5) 60.286   6) 50.131

7) 46.991   8) 69.362   9) 68.386

23

Answers of Rounding Decimals

✏️ **Round each decimal number to the nearest place indicated.**

1) 16.2̲43 ⇒ 16.2
2) 10.28̲5 ⇒ 10.28
3) 10̲.590 ⇒ 11
4) 14.6̲43 ⇒ 14.6
5) 15̲.637 ⇒ 16
6) 15.9̲11 ⇒ 15.9
7) 17.33̲1 ⇒ 17.33
8) 13.67̲6 ⇒ 13.68
9) 13̲.496 ⇒ 13

✏️ **Round each decimal to the nearest whole number.**

1) 5.351 ⇒ 5
2) 21.188 ⇒ 21
3) 23.633 ⇒ 24
4) 26.586 ⇒ 27
5) 31.491 ⇒ 31
6) 11.106 ⇒ 11
7) 19.209 ⇒ 19
8) 29.205 ⇒ 29
9) 8.601 ⇒ 9

✏️ **Round each decimal to the nearest tenth.**

1) 68.347 ⇒ 68.3
2) 41.266 ⇒ 41.3
3) 45.782 ⇒ 45.8
4) 55.532 ⇒ 55.5
5) 65.674 ⇒ 65.7
6) 61.333 ⇒ 61.3
7) 63.801 ⇒ 63.8
8) 64.394 ⇒ 64.4
9) 49.501 ⇒ 49.5

✏️ **Round each decimal to the nearest hundredth.**

1) 51.392 ⇒ 51.39
2) 63.708 ⇒ 63.71
3) 64.951 ⇒ 64.95
4) 66.152 ⇒ 66.15
5) 60.286 ⇒ 60.29
6) 50.131 ⇒ 50.13
7) 46.991 ⇒ 46.99
8) 69.362 ⇒ 69.36
9) 68.386 ⇒ 68.39

Multiplying and Dividing Decimals

✏️ Solve.

1) 67.8 × 34.1

2) 76.6 × 24.2

3) 27.8 × 17.3

4) 71.6 × 15.2

5) 45.4 × 11.7

6) 88.1 × 32.6

7) 81.3 × 28.2

8) 22.4 × 13.5

9) 61.2 × 23.8

10) 31.2 × 14.6

11) 22.1 × 16.1

12) 36.5 × 17.8

✏️ Solve.

1) 71.4 ÷ 58.4

2) 43.6 ÷ 34.2

3) 26.6 ÷ 6.2

4) 45.8 ÷ 27.4

5) 72.6 ÷ 18.7

6) 13.3 ÷ 2.4

7) 56.1 ÷ 24.3

8) 38.7 ÷ 31.1

Answers of Multiplying and Dividing Decimals

✏️ Solve.

1) 67.8 × 34.1 = 2311.98

2) 76.6 × 24.2 = 1853.72

3) 27.8 × 17.3 = 480.94

4) 71.6 × 15.2 = 1088.32

5) 45.4 × 11.7 = 531.18

6) 88.1 × 32.6 = 2872.06

7) 81.3 × 28.2 = 2292.66

8) 22.4 × 13.5 = 302.4

9) 61.2 × 23.8 = 1456.56

10) 31.2 × 14.6 = 455.52

11) 22.1 × 16.1 = 355.81

12) 36.5 × 17.8 = 649.7

✏️ Solve.

1) 71.4 ÷ 58.4 = 1.2226...

2) 43.6 ÷ 34.2 = 1.2749...

3) 26.6 ÷ 6.2 = 4.2903...

4) 45.8 ÷ 27.4 = 1.6715...

5) 72.6 ÷ 18.7 = 3.8824...

6) 13.3 ÷ 2.4 = 5.5417...

7) 56.1 ÷ 24.3 = 2.3086...

8) 38.7 ÷ 31.1 = 1.2444...

Converting Between Fractions, Decimals and Mixed Numbers

▷ **Convert fractions to decimals.**

1) $\frac{3}{10} =$ 2) $\frac{5}{3} =$ 3) $\frac{15}{1000} =$

4) $\frac{4}{7} =$ 5) $\frac{3}{19} =$ 6) $\frac{6}{3} =$

7) $\frac{4}{2} =$ 8) $\frac{6}{10} =$ 9) $\frac{14}{100} =$

10) $\frac{5}{2} =$ 11) $\frac{8}{14} =$ 12) $\frac{10}{1000} =$

13) $\frac{17}{10} =$ 14) $\frac{20}{1000} =$ 15) $\frac{3}{6} =$

▷ **Convert decimals to fractions.**

1) $0.34 =$ 2) $0.38 =$ 3) $0.81 =$

4) $0.25 =$ 5) $0.45 =$ 6) $0.13 =$

7) $0.14 =$ 8) $0.21 =$ 9) $0.44 =$

10) $0.31 =$ 11) $0.12 =$ 12) $0.47 =$

13) $0.43 =$ 14) $0.35 =$ 15) $0.17 =$

Answers of Converting Between Fractions, Decimals and Mixed Numbers

Convert fractions to decimals.

1) $\frac{3}{10} = 0.3$

2) $\frac{5}{3} = 1.667...$

3) $\frac{15}{1000} = 0.015$

4) $\frac{4}{7} = 0.571...$

5) $\frac{3}{19} = 0.158...$

6) $\frac{6}{3} = 2$

7) $\frac{4}{2} = 2$

8) $\frac{6}{10} = 0.6$

9) $\frac{14}{100} = 0.14$

10) $\frac{5}{2} = 2.5$

11) $\frac{8}{14} = 0.571...$

12) $\frac{10}{1000} = 0.01$

13) $\frac{17}{10} = 1.7$

14) $\frac{20}{1000} = 0.02$

15) $\frac{3}{6} = 0.5$

Convert decimals to fractions.

1) $0.34 = \frac{17}{50}$

2) $0.38 = \frac{19}{50}$

3) $0.81 = \frac{81}{100}$

4) $0.25 = \frac{1}{4}$

5) $0.45 = \frac{9}{20}$

6) $0.13 = \frac{13}{100}$

7) $0.14 = \frac{7}{50}$

8) $0.21 = \frac{21}{100}$

9) $0.44 = \frac{11}{25}$

10) $0.31 = \frac{31}{100}$

11) $0.12 = \frac{3}{25}$

12) $0.47 = \frac{47}{100}$

13) $0.43 = \frac{43}{100}$

14) $0.35 = \frac{7}{20}$

15) $0.17 = \frac{17}{100}$

Adding and Subtracting Integers

✏️ **Solve.**

1) $8 + (-23) - (-5) =$

2) $(-43) + 13 - (-9) =$

3) $(-47) + (-12) =$

4) $(-15) + (-13) + (-25) =$

5) $(-35) + (-24) =$

6) $24 + (-10) - (-27) =$

7) $(-7) + (-15) - (-7) =$

8) $21 + (-16) + (-22) =$

9) $(-2) + 7 + (-30) =$

10) $33 + (-11) =$

11) $7 + (-27) + (-26) =$

12) $(-46) + (-23) =$

13) $39 + 18 + (-14) =$

14) $10 + 6 + (-18) =$

15) $49 + 19 + (-14) =$

16) $(-1) + (-15) =$

17) $20 + 24 + (-28) =$

18) $(-33) + 24 - (-14) =$

19) $(-49) + (-6) + (-16) =$

20) $39 + (-8) - (-12) =$

21) $28 + (-27) - (-27) =$

22) $18 + (-8) + (-13) =$

Answers of Adding and Subtracting Integers

Solve.

1) $8 + (-23) - (-5) = -10$

2) $(-43) + 13 - (-9) = -21$

3) $(-47) + (-12) = -59$

4) $(-15) + (-13) + (-25) = -53$

5) $(-35) + (-24) = -59$

6) $24 + (-10) - (-27) = 41$

7) $(-7) + (-15) - (-7) = -15$

8) $21 + (-16) + (-22) = -17$

9) $(-2) + 7 + (-30) = -25$

10) $33 + (-11) = 22$

11) $7 + (-27) + (-26) = -46$

12) $(-46) + (-23) = -69$

13) $39 + 18 + (-14) = 43$

14) $10 + 6 + (-18) = -2$

15) $49 + 19 + (-14) = 54$

16) $(-1) + (-15) = -16$

17) $20 + 24 + (-28) = 16$

18) $(-33) + 24 - (-14) = 5$

19) $(-49) + (-6) + (-16) = -71$

20) $39 + (-8) - (-12) = 43$

21) $28 + (-27) - (-27) = 28$

22) $18 + (-8) + (-13) = -3$

Multiplying and Dividing Integers

✏️ **Get the result.**

1) $0 \div 0 =$

2) $9 \times 2 \times (-4) =$

3) $3 \times 1 \times (-4) =$

4) $(-8) \div (-4) =$

5) $9 \times 7 \times (-9) =$

6) $2 \times 1 \times (-7) =$

7) $(-6) \times 7 \times (-6) =$

8) $4 \times (-4) =$

9) $4 \times 4 =$

10) $(-4) \times (-5) =$

11) $5 \times (-5) =$

12) $10 \div 5 =$

13) $(-5) \times 4 \times (-9) =$

14) $1 \times (-9) \times (-10) =$

15) $(-9) \times 4 \times (-3) =$

16) $(-4) \times 4 =$

17) $(-24) \div 8 =$

18) $(-8) \times (-6) \times (-7) =$

19) $6 \times (-9) \times (-7) =$

20) $0 \times (-2) \times (-6) =$

21) $2 \times 1 =$

22) $(-1) \times 3 \times (-9) =$

Answers of Multiplying and Dividing Integers

✏️ **Get the result.**

1) $0 \div 0 = -4$

2) $9 \times 2 \times (-4) = -72$

3) $3 \times 1 \times (-4) = -12$

4) $(-8) \div (-4) = 2$

5) $9 \times 7 \times (-9) = -567$

6) $2 \times 1 \times (-7) = -14$

7) $(-6) \times 7 \times (-6) = 252$

8) $4 \times (-4) = -16$

9) $4 \times 4 = 16$

10) $(-4) \times (-5) = 20$

11) $5 \times (-5) = -25$

12) $10 \div 5 = 2$

13) $(-5) \times 4 \times (-9) = 180$

14) $1 \times (-9) \times (-10) = 90$

15) $(-9) \times 4 \times (-3) = 108$

16) $(-4) \times 4 = -16$

17) $(-24) \div 8 = -3$

18) $(-8) \times (-6) \times (-7) = -336$

19) $6 \times (-9) \times (-7) = 378$

20) $0 \times (-2) \times (-6) = 0$

21) $2 \times 1 = 2$

22) $(-1) \times 3 \times (-9) = 27$

Order of Operations

✏️ **Evaluate each expression.**

1) $(-9) \times 5 + 11 \times 4 =$

2) $6 \times 6 - 15 =$

3) $6 \times 4 - 12 =$

4) $49 \div 7 + 4 =$

5) $-24 \div 6 + 6 =$

6) $(-8) \times 1 + 5 =$

7) $64 \div 8 + 2 =$

8) $3 \times (-8) + 5 =$

9) $-32 \div 8 + 6 =$

10) $(-7) \times (-6) - 19 =$

11) $(-4) \times 2 + 2 =$

12) $(-8) \times (-2) - 10 =$

13) $8 \times (-8) - 13 =$

14) $9 \times 4 - 16 =$

15) $6 \times 4 - 20 =$

16) $2 \times 7 + 11 \times 3 =$

17) $0 \div 8 + 5 =$

18) $(-6) \times (-4) - 3 =$

19) $(-7) \times (-5) - 21 =$

20) $(-6) \times 9 + 18 =$

21) $-6 \div 6 + 7 =$

22) $(-3) \times 7 + 6 \times 6 =$

Answers of Order of Operations

✏️ **Evaluate each expression.**

1) $(-9) \times 5 + 11 \times 4 = -1$

2) $6 \times 6 - 15 = 21$

3) $6 \times 4 - 12 = 12$

4) $49 \div 7 + 4 = 11$

5) $-24 \div 6 + 6 = 2$

6) $(-8) \times 1 + 5 = -3$

7) $64 \div 8 + 2 = 10$

8) $3 \times (-8) + 5 = -19$

9) $-32 \div 8 + 6 = 2$

10) $(-7) \times (-6) - 19 = 23$

11) $(-4) \times 2 + 2 = -6$

12) $(-8) \times (-2) - 10 = 6$

13) $8 \times (-8) - 13 = -77$

14) $9 \times 4 - 16 = 20$

15) $6 \times 4 - 20 = 4$

16) $2 \times 7 + 11 \times 3 = 47$

17) $0 \div 8 + 5 = 5$

18) $(-6) \times (-4) - 3 = 21$

19) $(-7) \times (-5) - 21 = 14$

20) $(-6) \times 9 + 18 = -36$

21) $-6 \div 6 + 7 = 6$

22) $(-3) \times 7 + 6 \times 6 = 15$

Integers and Absolute Value

Solve.

1) $|14| =$
2) $|15| =$
3) $|16| =$
4) $|2| =$
5) $|-11| =$
6) $|-1| =$
7) $|-12| =$
8) $|-16| =$
9) $|-2| =$
10) $|20| =$
11) $|-18| =$
12) $|-4| =$
13) $|11| =$
14) $|-9| =$
15) $|18| =$
16) $|-8| =$
17) $|9| =$
18) $|10| =$

Evaluate.

1) $|-8| + |2| =$
2) $|-5| + |-8| =$
3) $|-11| + |4| =$
4) $6 + |3| =$
5) $-15 + |1| =$
6) $|-13| + |3| =$
7) $17 + |-7| =$
8) $-18 + |6| =$
9) $|17| + |-1| =$
10) $|7| + |-2| =$
11) $|-3| + |6| =$
12) $-2 + |-10| =$
13) $14 + |8| =$
14) $20 + |-3| =$
15) $11 + |-8| =$

Answers of Integers and Absolute Value

Solve.

1) $|14| = 14$
2) $|15| = 15$
3) $|16| = 16$
4) $|2| = 2$
5) $|-11| = 11$
6) $|-1| = 1$
7) $|-12| = 12$
8) $|-16| = 16$
9) $|-2| = 2$
10) $|20| = 20$
11) $|-18| = 18$
12) $|-4| = 4$
13) $|11| = 11$
14) $|-9| = 9$
15) $|18| = 18$
16) $|-8| = 8$
17) $|9| = 9$
18) $|10| = 10$

Evaluate.

1) $|-8| + |2| = 10$
2) $|-5| + |-8| = 13$
3) $|-11| + |4| = 15$
4) $6 + |3| = 9$
5) $-15 + |1| = -14$
6) $|-13| + |3| = 16$
7) $17 + |-7| = 24$
8) $-18 + |6| = -12$
9) $|17| + |-1| = 18$
10) $|7| + |-2| = 9$
11) $|-3| + |6| = 9$
12) $-2 + |-10| = 8$
13) $14 + |8| = 22$
14) $20 + |-3| = 23$
15) $11 + |-8| = 19$

Writing Ratios

✏️ **Express each ratio as a rate and unit rate.**

1) 126.00 dollars for 6 books

2) 55.00 dollars for 5 books

3) 117 inches of snow in 39 hours

4) 145.00 dollars for 5 books

5) 39 inches of snow in 13 hours

6) 112 inches of snow in 28 hours

7) 51.00 dollars for 3 books

8) 105.00 dollars for 3 books

9) 69 miles on 3 gallons of gas

10) 150 miles on 6 gallons of gas

✏️ **Express each ratio as a fraction in the simplest form.**

1) 40 miles out of 50 miles

2) 5 miles out of 25 miles

3) 36 miles out of 51 miles

4) 15 miles out of 33 miles

5) 24 miles out of 28 miles

6) 35 miles out of 45 miles

7) 55 miles out of 60 miles

8) 6 cakes out of 27 cakes

9) 17 dimes out of 51 coins

10) 25 cakes out of 35 cakes

Answers of Writing Ratios

✏️ **Express each ratio as a rate and unit rate.**

1) 126.00 dollars for 6 books ⇒ 21.00 dollars per book

2) 55.00 dollars for 5 books ⇒ 11.00 dollars per book

3) 117 inches of snow in 39 hours ⇒ 3 inches of snow per hour

4) 145.00 dollars for 5 books ⇒ 29.00 dollars per book

5) 39 inches of snow in 13 hours ⇒ 3 inches of snow per hour

6) 112 inches of snow in 28 hours ⇒ 4 inches of snow per hour

7) 51.00 dollars for 3 books ⇒ 17.00 dollars per book

8) 105.00 dollars for 3 books ⇒ 35.00 dollars per book

9) 69 miles on 3 gallons of gas ⇒ 23 miles per gallon

10) 150 miles on 6 gallons of gas ⇒ 25 miles per gallon

✏️ **Express each ratio as a fraction in the simplest form.**

1) 40 miles out of 50 miles ⇒ $\frac{4}{5}$

2) 5 miles out of 25 miles ⇒ $\frac{1}{5}$

3) 36 miles out of 51 miles ⇒ $\frac{12}{17}$

4) 15 miles out of 33 miles ⇒ $\frac{5}{11}$

5) 24 miles out of 28 miles ⇒ $\frac{6}{7}$

6) 35 miles out of 45 miles ⇒ $\frac{7}{9}$

7) 55 miles out of 60 miles ⇒ $\frac{11}{12}$

8) 6 cakes out of 27 cakes ⇒ $\frac{2}{9}$

9) 17 dimes out of 51 coins ⇒ $\frac{1}{3}$

10) 25 cakes out of 35 cakes ⇒ $\frac{5}{7}$

Simplifying Ratios

▶ **Reduce each ratio.**

1) $6 : 15 =$ 2) $8 : 52 =$ 3) $57 : 84 =$

4) $14 : 21 =$ 5) $6 : 30 =$ 6) $57 : 87 =$

7) $35 : 50 =$ 8) $3 : 69 =$ 9) $14 : 77 =$

10) $33 : 48 =$ 11) $69 : 75 =$ 12) $51 : 60 =$

13) $12 : 39 =$ 14) $39 : 90 =$ 15) $52 : 56 =$

▶ **Write each ratio as a fraction in simplest form.**

1) $3 : 12 =$ 2) $32 : 36 =$ 3) $32 : 76 =$

4) $12 : 21 =$ 5) $7 : 42 =$ 6) $16 : 32 =$

7) $9 : 87 =$ 8) $18 : 90 =$ 9) $32 : 72 =$

10) $40 : 48 =$ 11) $55 : 65 =$ 12) $57 : 81 =$

13) $30 : 54 =$ 14) $54 : 69 =$ 15) $35 : 63 =$

Answers of Simplifying Ratios

✏️ **Reduce each ratio.**

1) $6:15 = 2:5$
2) $8:52 = 2:13$
3) $57:84 = 19:28$

4) $14:21 = 2:3$
5) $6:30 = 1:5$
6) $57:87 = 19:29$

7) $35:50 = 7:10$
8) $3:69 = 1:23$
9) $14:77 = 2:11$

10) $33:48 = 11:16$
11) $69:75 = 23:25$
12) $51:60 = 17:20$

13) $12:39 = 4:13$
14) $39:90 = 13:30$
15) $52:56 = 13:14$

✏️ **Write each ratio as a fraction in simplest form.**

1) $3:12 = \frac{1}{4}$
2) $32:36 = \frac{8}{9}$
3) $32:76 = \frac{8}{19}$

4) $12:21 = \frac{4}{7}$
5) $7:42 = \frac{1}{6}$
6) $16:32 = \frac{1}{2}$

7) $9:87 = \frac{3}{29}$
8) $18:90 = \frac{1}{5}$
9) $32:72 = \frac{4}{9}$

10) $40:48 = \frac{5}{6}$
11) $55:65 = \frac{11}{13}$
12) $57:81 = \frac{19}{27}$

13) $30:54 = \frac{5}{9}$
14) $54:69 = \frac{18}{23}$
15) $35:63 = \frac{5}{9}$

Similar Figures

✏️ **Each pair of figures is similar. Find the missing side.**

1) $x =$
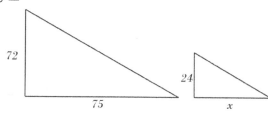

2) $x =$
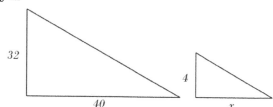

3) $x =$
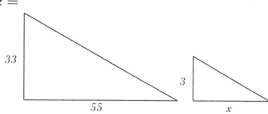

4) $x =$
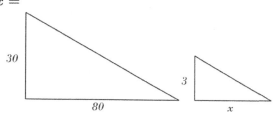

5) $x =$
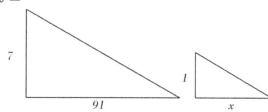

6) $x =$
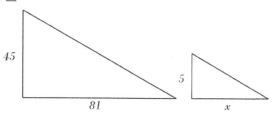

7) $x =$
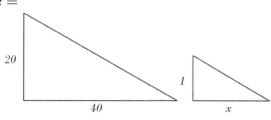

8) $x =$
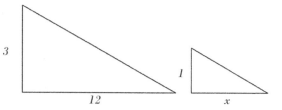

Answers of Similar Figures

 Each pair of figures is similar. Find the missing side.

1) $x = 25$

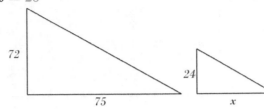

2) $x = 5$

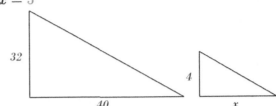

3) $x = 5$

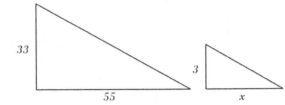

4) $x = 8$

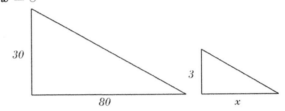

5) $x = 13$

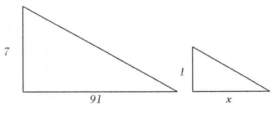

6) $x = 9$

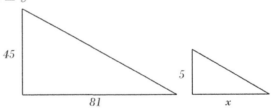

7) $x = 2$

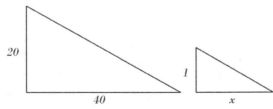

8) $x = 4$

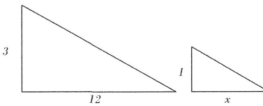

Proportional Ratios

✏️ **Fill in the blanks; solve each proportion.**

1) $16 : 88 = \_\_ : 11$
2) $25 : 30 = \_\_ : 6$
3) $6 : 81 = \_\_ : 27$

4) $15 : 75 = 1 : \_\_$
5) $56 : 76 = \_\_ : 19$
6) $10 : 35 = \_\_ : 7$

7) $22 : 55 = 2 : \_\_$
8) $8 : 16 = \_\_ : 2$
9) $6 : 21 = \_\_ : 7$

10) $12 : 28 = \_\_ : 7$
11) $15 : 87 = \_\_ : 29$
12) $13 : 26 = 1 : \_\_$

13) $21 : 60 = 7 : \_\_$
14) $28 : 32 = \_\_ : 8$
15) $24 : 27 = \_\_ : 9$

16) $70 : 80 = 7 : \_\_$
17) $6 : 93 = 2 : \_\_$
18) $15 : 51 = 5 : \_\_$

19) $15 : 20 = \_\_ : 4$
20) $16 : 24 = \_\_ : 3$
21) $24 : 39 = \_\_ : 13$

22) $49 : 56 = 7 : \_\_$
23) $48 : 76 = 12 : \_\_$
24) $3 : 63 = \_\_ : 21$

25) $48 : 92 = 12 : \_\_$
26) $76 : 80 = \_\_ : 20$
27) $75 : 84 = \_\_ : 28$

28) $63 : 77 = \_\_ : 11$
29) $20 : 65 = \_\_ : 13$
30) $20 : 36 = \_\_ : 9$

31) $21 : 57 = 7 : \_\_$
32) $6 : 33 = 2 : \_\_$
33) $85 : 90 = 17 : \_\_$

Answers of Proportional Ratios

✏️ **Fill in the blanks; solve each proportion.**

1) $16:88 = 2:11$ 2) $25:30 = 5:6$ 3) $6:81 = 2:27$

4) $15:75 = 1:5$ 5) $56:76 = 14:19$ 6) $10:35 = 2:7$

7) $22:55 = 2:5$ 8) $8:16 = 1:2$ 9) $6:21 = 2:7$

10) $12:28 = 3:7$ 11) $15:87 = 5:29$ 12) $13:26 = 1:2$

13) $21:60 = 7:20$ 14) $28:32 = 7:8$ 15) $24:27 = 8:9$

16) $70:80 = 7:8$ 17) $6:93 = 2:31$ 18) $15:51 = 5:17$

19) $15:20 = 3:4$ 20) $16:24 = 2:3$ 21) $24:39 = 8:13$

22) $49:56 = 7:8$ 23) $48:76 = 12:19$ 24) $3:63 = 1:21$

25) $48:92 = 12:23$ 26) $76:80 = 19:20$ 27) $75:84 = 25:28$

28) $63:77 = 9:11$ 29) $20:65 = 4:13$ 30) $20:36 = 5:9$

31) $21:57 = 7:19$ 32) $6:33 = 2:11$ 33) $85:90 = 17:18$

Percentage Calculations

✏️ **Calculate the percentages.**

1) 95% of 87 =

2) 45% of 59 =

3) 80% of 72 =

4) 60% of 46 =

5) 65% of 96 =

6) 25% of 33 =

7) 40% of 22 =

8) 85% of 98 =

9) 90% of 66 =

10) 75% of 70 =

✏️ **Solve.**

1) 51.1 is what percentage of 73?

2) 5.5 is what percentage of 22?

3) 68.25 is what percentage of 91?

4) 54.15 is what percentage of 57?

5) 16.8 is what percentage of 56?

6) 46.8 is what percentage of 72?

7) 27.3 is what percentage of 39?

8) 15.3 is what percentage of 34?

9) 9.45 is what percentage of 27?

10) 72.75 is what percentage of 97?

11) 37.95 is what percentage of 69?

12) 53.25 is what percentage of 71?

Answers of Percentage Calculations

✏️ **Calculate the percentages.**

1) 95% of 87 = 82.65

2) 45% of 59 = 26.55

3) 80% of 72 = 57.6

4) 60% of 46 = 27.6

5) 65% of 96 = 62.4

6) 25% of 33 = 8.25

7) 40% of 22 = 8.8

8) 85% of 98 = 83.3

9) 90% of 66 = 59.4

10) 75% of 70 = 52.5

✏️ **Solve.**

1) 51.1 is what percentage of 73? 70%

2) 5.5 is what percentage of 22? 25%

3) 68.25 is what percentage of 91? 75%

4) 54.15 is what percentage of 57? 95%

5) 16.8 is what percentage of 56? 30%

6) 46.8 is what percentage of 72? 65%

7) 27.3 is what percentage of 39? 70%

8) 15.3 is what percentage of 34? 45%

9) 9.45 is what percentage of 27? 35%

10) 72.75 is what percentage of 97? 75%

11) 37.95 is what percentage of 69? 55%

12) 53.25 is what percentage of 71? 75%

Converting Between Percent, Fractions, and Decimals

✏️ **Converting fractions to decimals.**

1) $\frac{85}{100}=$ 2) $\frac{30}{100}=$

3) $\frac{65}{100}=$ 4) $\frac{45}{100}=$

5) $\frac{25}{100}=$ 6) $\frac{50}{100}=$

7) $\frac{80}{100}=$ 8) $\frac{15}{100}=$

9) $\frac{40}{100}=$ 10) $\frac{90}{100}=$

✏️ **Write each decimal as a percent.**

1) $0.665=$ 2) $0.34=$

3) $0.66=$ 4) $0.18=$

5) $0.425=$ 6) $0.295=$

7) $0.315=$ 8) $0.845=$

9) $0.31=$ 10) $0.52=$

11) $0.45=$ 12) $0.875=$

Answers of Converting Between Percent, Fractions, and Decimals

✏️ **Converting fractions to decimals.**

1) $\frac{85}{100} = 0.85$

2) $\frac{30}{100} = 0.3$

3) $\frac{65}{100} = 0.65$

4) $\frac{45}{100} = 0.45$

5) $\frac{25}{100} = 0.25$

6) $\frac{50}{100} = 0.5$

7) $\frac{80}{100} = 0.8$

8) $\frac{15}{100} = 0.15$

9) $\frac{40}{100} = 0.4$

10) $\frac{90}{100} = 0.9$

✏️ **Write each decimal as a percent.**

1) $0.665 = 66.5\%$

2) $0.34 = 34\%$

3) $0.66 = 66\%$

4) $0.18 = 18\%$

5) $0.425 = 42.5\%$

6) $0.295 = 29.5\%$

7) $0.315 = 31.5\%$

8) $0.845 = 84.5\%$

9) $0.31 = 31\%$

10) $0.52 = 52\%$

11) $0.45 = 45\%$

12) $0.875 = 87.5\%$

Percent Problems

Solve each problem.

1) 92 is 736% of what?

2) 58 is 174% of what?

3) What percent of 70 is 14.28?

4) What percent of 60 is 33.33?

5) What percent of 62 is 11.11?

6) 98 is 490% of what?

7) 54 is 378% of what?

8) 62 is 124% of what?

9) 78 is 624% of what?

10) What percent of 88 is 11.11?

11) 72 is 576% of what?

12) 88 is 792% of what?

13) 68 is 136% of what?

14) What percent of 54 is 20?

15) 84 is 588% of what?

16) What percent of 66 is 33.33?

17) 74 is 296% of what?

18) 60 is 600% of what?

19) What percent of 74 is 25?

20) What percent of 80 is 11.11?

21) What percent of 82 is 10?

22) 76 is 228% of what?

Answers of Percent Problems

✏️ **Solve each problem.**

1) 92 is 736% of what? 12.5

2) 58 is 174% of what? 33.33

3) What percent of 70 is 14.28? 20.39%

4) What percent of 60 is 33.33? 55.55%

5) What percent of 62 is 11.11? 17.91%

6) 98 is 490% of what? 20

7) 54 is 378% of what? 14.28

8) 62 is 124% of what? 50

9) 78 is 624% of what? 12.5

10) What percent of 88 is 11.11? 12.62%

11) 72 is 576% of what? 12.5

12) 88 is 792% of what? 11.11

13) 68 is 136% of what? 50

14) What percent of 54 is 20? 37.03%

15) 84 is 588% of what? 14.28

16) What percent of 66 is 33.33? 50.5%

17) 74 is 296% of what? 25

18) 60 is 600% of what? 10

19) What percent of 74 is 25? 33.78%

20) What percent of 80 is 11.11? 13.88%

21) What percent of 82 is 10? 12.19%

22) 76 is 228% of what? 33.33

Markup, Discount, and Tax

✏️ **Find the selling price of each item.**

1) Cost of a watch $21.3, markup: 63%, discount: 57%, tax: 7% :

2) Cost of a bag $24, markup: 30%, discount: 49%, tax: 6% :

3) Cost of a bag $15, markup: 44%, discount: 49%, tax: 9% :

4) Cost of a bag $33.1, markup: 65%, discount: 55%, tax: 6% :

5) Cost of a belt $8, markup: 26%, discount: 38%, tax: 5% :

6) Cost of a shirt $27.69, markup: 72%, discount: 52%, tax: 8% :

7) Cost of a wallet $25.48, markup: 77%, discount: 66%, tax: 9% :

8) Cost of a shirt $9.65, markup: 79%, discount: 69%, tax: 5% :

9) Cost of a toy $31, markup: 46%, discount: 10%, tax: 8% :

10) Cost of a toy $22, markup: 20%, discount: 35%, tax: 8% :

11) Cost of a hat $23, markup: 32%, discount: 30%, tax: 7% :

12) Cost of a bag $15.81, markup: 68%, discount: 73%, tax: 5% :

13) Cost of a shirt $9, markup: 48%, discount: 20%, tax: 8% :

Answers of Markup, Discount, and Tax

✏️ **Find the selling price of each item.**

1) Cost of a watch $21.3, markup: 63%, discount: 57%, tax: 7% : 15.97

2) Cost of a bag $24, markup: 30%, discount: 49%, tax: 6% : 16.87

3) Cost of a bag $15, markup: 44%, discount: 49%, tax: 9% : 12.01

4) Cost of a bag $33.1, markup: 65%, discount: 55%, tax: 6% : 26.05

5) Cost of a belt $8, markup: 26%, discount: 38%, tax: 5% : 6.56

6) Cost of a shirt $27.69, markup: 72%, discount: 52%, tax: 8% : 24.68

7) Cost of a wallet $25.48, markup: 77%, discount: 66%, tax: 9% : 16.72

8) Cost of a shirt $9.65, markup: 79%, discount: 69%, tax: 5% : 5.62

9) Cost of a toy $31, markup: 46%, discount: 10%, tax: 8% : 43.99

10) Cost of a toy $22, markup: 20%, discount: 35%, tax: 8% : 18.54

11) Cost of a hat $23, markup: 32%, discount: 30%, tax: 7% : 22.74

12) Cost of a bag $15.81, markup: 68%, discount: 73%, tax: 5% : 7.53

13) Cost of a shirt $9, markup: 48%, discount: 20%, tax: 8% : 11.51

Simple Interest

✏️ **Use simple interest to find the ending balance.**

1) $4,400.00 at 13% for 6 years.

2) $2,150.00 at 16% for 10 years.

3) $2,550.00 at 10% for 4 years.

4) $4,850.00 at 14% for 6 years.

5) $4,200.00 at 19% for 4 years.

6) $4,550.00 at 16% for 6 years.

7) $2,600.00 at 18% for 6 years.

8) $4,650.00 at 6% for 13 years.

9) $4,600.00 at 9% for 3 years.

10) $5,500.00 at 8% for 14 years.

11) $3,400.00 at 2% for 14 years.

12) $3,150.00 at 16% for 11 years.

13) $1,950.00 at 11% for 12 years.

14) $1,450.00 at 10% for 4 years.

15) $5,350.00 at 19% for 14 years.

16) $4,450.00 at 4% for 5 years.

17) $4,700.00 at 13% for 13 years.

18) $1,200.00 at 3% for 9 years.

19) $1,350.00 at 17% for 14 years.

20) $2,800.00 at 10% for 11 years.

21) $4,100.00 at 10% for 10 years.

22) $2,950.00 at 9% for 10 years.

Answers of Simple Interest

✏️ Use simple interest to find the ending balance.

1) $4,400.00 at 13% for 6 years.
   ⇒ $7,832.00

2) $2,150.00 at 16% for 10 years.
   ⇒ $5,590.00

3) $2,550.00 at 10% for 4 years.
   ⇒ $3,570.00

4) $4,850.00 at 14% for 6 years.
   ⇒ $8,924.00

5) $4,200.00 at 19% for 4 years.
   ⇒ $7,392.00

6) $4,550.00 at 16% for 6 years.
   ⇒ $8,918.00

7) $2,600.00 at 18% for 6 years.
   ⇒ $5,408.00

8) $4,650.00 at 6% for 13 years.
   ⇒ $8,277.00

9) $4,600.00 at 9% for 3 years.
   ⇒ $5,842.00

10) $5,500.00 at 8% for 14 years.
    ⇒ $11,660.00

11) $3,400.00 at 2% for 14 years.
    ⇒ $4,352.00

12) $3,150.00 at 16% for 11 years.
    ⇒ $8,694.00

13) $1,950.00 at 11% for 12 years.
    ⇒ $4,524.00

14) $1,450.00 at 10% for 4 years.
    ⇒ $2,030.00

15) $5,350.00 at 19% for 14 years.
    ⇒ $19,581.00

16) $4,450.00 at 4% for 5 years.
    ⇒ $5,340.00

17) $4,700.00 at 13% for 13 years.
    ⇒ $12,643.00

18) $1,200.00 at 3% for 9 years.
    ⇒ $1,524.00

19) $1,350.00 at 17% for 14 years.
    ⇒ $4,563.00

20) $2,800.00 at 10% for 11 years.
    ⇒ $5,880.00

21) $4,100.00 at 10% for 10 years.
    ⇒ $8,200.00

22) $2,950.00 at 9% for 10 years.
    ⇒ $5,605.00

Expressions and Variables

✏️ **Simplify each expression.**

1) $x + 4x - x$, use $x = 6$

2) $x + x(5x - x)$, use $x = 5$

3) $x + 20x - x$, use $x = 7$

4) $x + 21x$, use $x = 1$

5) $10 + x(9x - x)$, use $x = 4$

6) $x + 10x$, use $x = 5$

7) $x + 2x - x$, use $x = 1$

8) $10 + x(13x - x)$, use $x = 1$

9) $x + 3x$, use $x = 2$

10) $x + 14x - x$, use $x = 8$

11) $x + 13x$, use $x = 5$

12) $10 + x(2x - x)$, use $x = 3$

13) $x + 9x$, use $x = 8$

14) $x + 11x - x$, use $x = 6$

15) $x + 2x$, use $x = 3$

16) $x + 18x - x$, use $x = 1$

17) $x + 19x - x$, use $x = 5$

18) $x + x(20x - x)$, use $x = 4$

19) $x + x(8x - x)$, use $x = 5$

20) $x + 3x - x$, use $x = 7$

21) $x + x(12x - x)$, use $x = 7$

22) $10 + x(7x - x)$, use $x = 3$

Answers of Expressions and Variables

✏️ **Simplify each expression.**

1) $x + 4x - x = 24$, use $x = 6$

2) $x + x(5x - x) = 105$, use $x = 5$

3) $x + 20x - x = 140$, use $x = 7$

4) $x + 21x = 22$, use $x = 1$

5) $10 + x(9x - x) = 138$, use $x = 4$

6) $x + 10x = 55$, use $x = 5$

7) $x + 2x - x = 2$, use $x = 1$

8) $10 + x(13x - x) = 22$, use $x = 1$

9) $x + 3x = 8$, use $x = 2$

10) $x + 14x - x = 112$, use $x = 8$

11) $x + 13x = 70$, use $x = 5$

12) $10 + x(2x - x) = 19$, use $x = 3$

13) $x + 9x = 80$, use $x = 8$

14) $x + 11x - x = 66$, use $x = 6$

15) $x + 2x = 9$, use $x = 3$

16) $x + 18x - x = 18$, use $x = 1$

17) $x + 19x - x = 95$, use $x = 5$

18) $x + x(20x - x) = 308$, use $x = 4$

19) $x + x(8x - x) = 180$, use $x = 5$

20) $x + 3x - x = 21$, use $x = 7$

21) $x + x(12x - x) = 546$, use $x = 7$

22) $10 + x(7x - x) = 64$, use $x = 3$

Simplifying Variable Expressions

✏️ **Simplify each expression.**

1) $5x^2(5x + x) - x^3 =$

2) $21x + 7x^2 =$

3) $16x + 2x^2 =$

4) $3x^2(5x + x) + x^3 =$

5) $11x^2(5x + x) + x^3 =$

6) $4x^2(2x + x) - x^3 =$

7) $8x^2(2x) =$

8) $5x + 4x^2 =$

9) $16x^2(6x + x) =$

10) $6x + 4x^2 =$

11) $8x^2(6x + x) - x^3 =$

12) $12x + 6x^2 =$

13) $17x^2(3x + x) =$

14) $12x^2(2x + x) =$

15) $14x^2(6x + x) - x^3 =$

16) $10x + 7x^2 =$

17) $18x^2(5x) =$

18) $2x^2(4x) =$

19) $12x^2(5x + x) + x^3 =$

20) $15x^2(4x + x) =$

21) $15x^2(2x + x) - x^3 =$

22) $14x^2(4x + x) =$

Answers of Simplifying Variable Expressions

✏️ **Simplify each expression.**

1) $5x^2(5x + x) - x^3 = 29x^3$

2) $21x + 7x^2 = x(21 + 7x)$

3) $16x + 2x^2 = x(16 + 2x)$

4) $3x^2(5x + x) + x^3 = 19x^3$

5) $11x^2(5x + x) + x^3 = 67x^3$

6) $4x^2(2x + x) - x^3 = 11x^3$

7) $8x^2(2x) = 16x^3$

8) $5x + 4x^2 = x(5 + 4x)$

9) $16x^2(6x + x) = 112x^3$

10) $6x + 4x^2 = x(6 + 4x)$

11) $8x^2(6x + x) - x^3 = 55x^3$

12) $12x + 6x^2 = x(12 + 6x)$

13) $17x^2(3x + x) = 68x^3$

14) $12x^2(2x + x) = 36x^3$

15) $14x^2(6x + x) - x^3 = 97x^3$

16) $10x + 7x^2 = x(10 + 7x)$

17) $18x^2(5x) = 90x^3$

18) $2x^2(4x) = 8x^3$

19) $12x^2(5x + x) + x^3 = 73x^3$

20) $15x^2(4x + x) = 75x^3$

21) $15x^2(2x + x) - x^3 = 44x^3$

22) $14x^2(4x + x) = 70x^3$

Simplifying Polynomial Expressions

✏️ Simplify each polynomial.

1) $6x + 4x^2 + x^3 + 7x - 7 =$

2) $13x^3 + 7x^2 - 4x^3 + 17x^2 - 20x^3 + 11x^2 =$

3) $11x + 3x^2 - x^3 + 5x =$

4) $19x + 6x^2 - x^3 + 3x =$

5) $(20x^3 + 7x^2 - 5x^3) + (25x^2 - 27x^3 + 12x^2) =$

6) $(8x^3 + 6x^2 - 4x^3) + (12x^2 - 14x^3 + 10x^2) =$

7) $5x^3 + 6x^2 - 3x^3 + 8x^2 - 11x^3 + 9x^2 =$

8) $(10x^3 + 5x^2 - 5x^3) + (15x^2 - 15x^3 + 10x^2) =$

9) $(11x^3 + 6x^2 - 4x^3) + (15x^2 - 17x^3 + 10x^2) =$

10) $(9x^3 + 2x^2 - 7x^3) + (16x^2 - 11x^3 + 9x^2) =$

11) $8x + 2x^2 - x^3 + 5x =$

Answers of Simplifying Polynomial Expressions

📝 **Simplify each polynomial.**

1) $6x + 4x^2 + x^3 + 7x - 7 = x^3 + 4x^2 + 13x - 7$

2) $13x^3 + 7x^2 - 4x^3 + 17x^2 - 20x^3 + 11x^2 = -11x^3 + 35x^2$

3) $11x + 3x^2 - x^3 + 5x = -x^3 + 3x^2 + 16x$

4) $19x + 6x^2 - x^3 + 3x = -x^3 + 6x^2 + 22x$

5) $(20x^3 + 7x^2 - 5x^3) + (25x^2 - 27x^3 + 12x^2) = -12x^3 + 44x^2$

6) $(8x^3 + 6x^2 - 4x^3) + (12x^2 - 14x^3 + 10x^2) = -10x^3 + 28x^2$

7) $5x^3 + 6x^2 - 3x^3 + 8x^2 - 11x^3 + 9x^2 = -9x^3 + 23x^2$

8) $(10x^3 + 5x^2 - 5x^3) + (15x^2 - 15x^3 + 10x^2) = -10x^3 + 30x^2$

9) $(11x^3 + 6x^2 - 4x^3) + (15x^2 - 17x^3 + 10x^2) = -10x^3 + 31x^2$

10) $(9x^3 + 2x^2 - 7x^3) + (16x^2 - 11x^3 + 9x^2) = -9x^3 + 27x^2$

11) $8x + 2x^2 - x^3 + 5x = -x^3 + 2x^2 + 13x$

The Distributive Property

✏️ **Use the distributive property to simplify each expression.**

1) $13(15 + 4x) =$

2) $-13(13 + 3x) =$

3) $-5(6 + 8x) =$

4) $-15(17 - 3x) =$

5) $-(-19 - 2x) =$

6) $-(7 - 4x) =$

7) $-3(9 - 7x) =$

8) $20(20 + 2x) =$

9) $-15(20 + 8x) =$

10) $-6(3 - 8x) =$

11) $-17(19 - 3x) =$

12) $-(-3 - 6x) =$

13) $-5(5 + 7x) =$

14) $12(18 + 8x) =$

15) $-(-5 - 3x) =$

16) $-(-18 - 7x) =$

17) $-10(10 + 3x) =$

18) $-(13 - 3x) =$

19) $2(7 + 7x) =$

20) $-5(12 - 8x) =$

21) $-(-12 - 6x) =$

22) $-(-20 - 3x) =$

Answers of The Distributive Property

✏️ Use the distributive property to simplify each expression.

1) $13(15 + 4x) = 52x + 195$

2) $-13(13 + 3x) = -39x - 169$

3) $-5(6 + 8x) = -40x - 30$

4) $-15(17 - 3x) = 45x - 255$

5) $-(-19 - 2x) = 2x + 19$

6) $-(7 - 4x) = 4x - 7$

7) $-3(9 - 7x) = 21x - 27$

8) $20(20 + 2x) = 40x + 400$

9) $-15(20 + 8x) = -120x - 300$

10) $-6(3 - 8x) = 48x - 18$

11) $-17(19 - 3x) = 51x - 323$

12) $-(-3 - 6x) = 6x + 3$

13) $-5(5 + 7x) = -35x - 25$

14) $12(18 + 8x) = 96x + 216$

15) $-(-5 - 3x) = 3x + 5$

16) $-(-18 - 7x) = 7x + 18$

17) $-10(10 + 3x) = -30x - 100$

18) $-(13 - 3x) = 3x - 13$

19) $2(7 + 7x) = 14x + 14$

20) $-5(12 - 8x) = 40x - 60$

21) $-(-12 - 6x) = 6x + 12$

22) $-(-20 - 3x) = 3x + 20$

Evaluating One Variable

✏️ **Simplify each algebraic expression.**

1) $x = 4,\ 7x + 3 =$

2) $x = 7,\ 2(\frac{21}{x} + 3) =$

3) $x = -20,\ \frac{40}{x} + 3 =$

4) $x = 14,\ 3(\frac{56}{x} + 7) =$

5) $x = -4,\ \frac{8}{x} + 2 =$

6) $x = 9,\ 2x + 7 =$

7) $x = 13,\ 4(\frac{26}{x} - 2) =$

8) $x = 12,\ \frac{48}{x} + 6 =$

9) $x = 2,\ 2(\frac{8}{x} + 3) =$

10) $x = -13,\ \frac{52}{x} + 5 =$

11) $x = 7,\ 7x - 4 =$

12) $x = -21,\ 4x + 4 =$

13) $x = 20,\ 3(\frac{60}{x} - 2) =$

14) $x = 8,\ 4(\frac{24}{x} + 2) =$

15) $x = -3,\ \frac{12}{x} + 8 =$

16) $x = 6,\ 2(\frac{12}{x} - 6) =$

17) $x = 18,\ \frac{72}{x} + 4 =$

18) $x = 11,\ x - 5 =$

19) $x = 2,\ 4x + 8 =$

20) $x = -9,\ \frac{27}{x} + 6 =$

21) $x = 21,\ 3(\frac{84}{x} - 2) =$

22) $x = 16,\ 3x + 2 =$

Answers of Evaluating One Variable

✏️ **Simplify each algebraic expression.**

1) $x = 4$, $7x + 3 = 31$

2) $x = 7$, $2(\frac{21}{x} + 3) = 12$

3) $x = -20$, $\frac{40}{x} + 3 = 1$

4) $x = 14$, $3(\frac{56}{x} + 7) = 33$

5) $x = -4$, $\frac{8}{x} + 2 = 0$

6) $x = 9$, $2x + 7 = 25$

7) $x = 13$, $4(\frac{26}{x} - 2) = 0$

8) $x = 12$, $\frac{48}{x} + 6 = 10$

9) $x = 2$, $2(\frac{8}{x} + 3) = 14$

10) $x = -13$, $\frac{52}{x} + 5 = 1$

11) $x = 7$, $7x - 4 = 45$

12) $x = -21$, $4x + 4 = -80$

13) $x = 20$, $3(\frac{60}{x} - 2) = 3$

14) $x = 8$, $4(\frac{24}{x} + 2) = 20$

15) $x = -3$, $\frac{12}{x} + 8 = 4$

16) $x = 6$, $2(\frac{12}{x} - 6) = -8$

17) $x = 18$, $\frac{72}{x} + 4 = 8$

18) $x = 11$, $x - 5 = 6$

19) $x = 2$, $4x + 8 = 16$

20) $x = -9$, $\frac{27}{x} + 6 = 3$

21) $x = 21$, $3(\frac{84}{x} - 2) = 6$

22) $x = 16$, $3x + 2 = 50$

Evaluating Two Variables

✏️ **Simplify each algebraic expression.**

1) $x = 11, y = 4,\ -4(3x - 4y - 11) =$

2) $x = 3, y = 2,\ 3x + 6y - 3 =$

3) $x = 5, y = 7,\ 4x + 20y - 5 =$

4) $x = 14, y = 3,\ 4x(2y - 14) =$

5) $x = 8, y = 3,\ 4x(3y - 8) =$

6) $x = 8, y = 4,\ 2x(2y - 8) =$

7) $x = 19, y = 4,\ 2x + \frac{12}{y} - 19 =$

8) $x = 10, y = 4,\ 4x(3y - 10) =$

9) $x = 12, y = 5,\ -5(2x - 3y - 12) =$

10) $x = 15, y = 4,\ 4(4x - 3y + 15) =$

11) $x = 10, y = 3,\ 2x + 20y - 10 =$

12) $x = 7, y = 5,\ 2x(3y - 7) =$

13) $x = 14, y = 5,\ 4x + 42y - 14 =$

Answers of Evaluating Two Variables

✏️ **Simplify each algebraic expression.**

1) $x = 11, y = 4, \ -4(3x - 4y - 11) = -24$

2) $x = 3, y = 2, \ 3x + 6y - 3 = 18$

3) $x = 5, y = 7, \ 4x + 20y - 5 = 155$

4) $x = 14, y = 3, \ 4x(2y - 14) = -448$

5) $x = 8, y = 3, \ 4x(3y - 8) = 32$

6) $x = 8, y = 4, \ 2x(2y - 8) = 0$

7) $x = 19, y = 4, \ 2x + \frac{12}{y} - 19 = 22$

8) $x = 10, y = 4, \ 4x(3y - 10) = 80$

9) $x = 12, y = 5, \ -5(2x - 3y - 12) = 15$

10) $x = 15, y = 4, \ 4(4x - 3y + 15) = 252$

11) $x = 10, y = 3, \ 2x + 20y - 10 = 70$

12) $x = 7, y = 5, \ 2x(3y - 7) = 112$

13) $x = 14, y = 5, \ 4x + 42y - 14 = 252$

Combining like Terms

➡ **Simplify each expression.**

1) $9x - 3x =$

2) $4x + 3(2x - 3 + x) =$

3) $9x + (4x - 3 - x) =$

4) $13x + (-3)(2x - 3 + x) =$

5) $6x - 14x =$

6) $10x + 4x - 3 =$

7) $4x + (3x - 5 - x) =$

8) $3x + 2(4x - 2 + x) =$

9) $7x + (5x - 2 - x) =$

10) $16x + 2(5x - 2 + x) =$

11) $14x + 2x - 2 =$

12) $10x + (-4)(4x - 4 + x) =$

13) $8x + (3x - 3 - x) =$

Answers of Combining like Terms

✏️ **Simplify each expression.**

1) $9x - 3x = 6x$

2) $4x + 3(2x - 3 + x) = 13x - 9$

3) $9x + (4x - 3 - x) = 12x - 3$

4) $13x + (-3)(2x - 3 + x) = 4x + 9$

5) $6x - 14x = -8x$

6) $10x + 4x - 3 = 14x - 3$

7) $4x + (3x - 5 - x) = 6x - 5$

8) $3x + 2(4x - 2 + x) = 13x - 4$

9) $7x + (5x - 2 - x) = 11x - 2$

10) $16x + 2(5x - 2 + x) = 28x - 4$

11) $14x + 2x - 2 = 16x - 2$

12) $10x + (-4)(4x - 4 + x) = -10x + 16$

13) $8x + (3x - 3 - x) = 10x - 3$

One Step Equations

✏️ **Solve each equation.**

1) $x + 3 = -1$

2) $x + 2 = -4$

3) $x + 4 = -6$

4) $x + 5 = 11$

5) $x - 2 = 10$

6) $x - 3 = -2$

7) $x + 5 = -3$

8) $x - 5 = 8$

9) $x - 4 = 4$

10) $x - 5 = -5$

11) $x - 3 = -1$

12) $x + 4 = 0$

13) $x - 4 = 0$

14) $x + 2 = 7$

15) $x - 4 = 6$

16) $x - 4 = 1$

17) $x + 2 = -7$

18) $x + 4 = -8$

19) $x - 3 = 9$

20) $x - 2 = -3$

21) $x - 5 = 2$

22) $x + 4 = 6$

Answers of One Step Equations

✏️ **Solve each equation.**

1) $x + 3 = -1 \Rightarrow x = -4$

2) $x + 2 = -4 \Rightarrow x = -6$

3) $x + 4 = -6 \Rightarrow x = -10$

4) $x + 5 = 11 \Rightarrow x = 6$

5) $x - 2 = 10 \Rightarrow x = 12$

6) $x - 3 = -2 \Rightarrow x = 1$

7) $x + 5 = -3 \Rightarrow x = -8$

8) $x - 5 = 8 \Rightarrow x = 13$

9) $x - 4 = 4 \Rightarrow x = 8$

10) $x - 5 = -5 \Rightarrow x = 0$

11) $x - 3 = -1 \Rightarrow x = 2$

12) $x + 4 = 0 \Rightarrow x = -4$

13) $x - 4 = 0 \Rightarrow x = 4$

14) $x + 2 = 7 \Rightarrow x = 5$

15) $x - 4 = 6 \Rightarrow x = 10$

16) $x - 4 = 1 \Rightarrow x = 5$

17) $x + 2 = -7 \Rightarrow x = -9$

18) $x + 4 = -8 \Rightarrow x = -12$

19) $x - 3 = 9 \Rightarrow x = 12$

20) $x - 2 = -3 \Rightarrow x = -1$

21) $x - 5 = 2 \Rightarrow x = 7$

22) $x + 4 = 6 \Rightarrow x = 2$

Two Step Equations

Solve each equation.

1) $3x - 12 = 24$

2) $3(x - 12) = 15$

3) $\frac{5x - 10}{3} = 100$

4) $4(x - 12) = 60$

5) $\frac{7x - 21}{5} = 70$

6) $4x - 12 = 24$

7) $3x - 12 = -12$

8) $\frac{4x - 8}{2} = 76$

9) $2(x - 8) = 12$

10) $\frac{2x - 8}{4} = 34$

11) $4(x - 12) = 40$

12) $\frac{5x - 20}{6} = 80$

13) $3x - 15 = -6$

14) $3x - 15 = 3$

15) $\frac{5x - 20}{6} = 60$

16) $3x - 6 = 12$

17) $\frac{5x - 25}{2} = 40$

18) $3x - 9 = -15$

19) $\frac{3x - 12}{4} = 42$

20) $\frac{2x - 6}{5} = 14$

21) $\frac{3x - 6}{3} = 12$

22) $3x - 6 = 27$

Answers of Two Step Equations

✏️ Solve each equation.

1) $3x - 12 = 24 \Rightarrow x = 12$

2) $3(x - 12) = 15 \Rightarrow x = 17$

3) $\frac{5x - 10}{3} = 100 \Rightarrow x = 62$

4) $4(x - 12) = 60 \Rightarrow x = 27$

5) $\frac{7x - 21}{5} = 70 \Rightarrow x = 53$

6) $4x - 12 = 24 \Rightarrow x = 9$

7) $3x - 12 = -12 \Rightarrow x = 0$

8) $\frac{4x - 8}{2} = 76 \Rightarrow x = 40$

9) $2(x - 8) = 12 \Rightarrow x = 14$

10) $\frac{2x - 8}{4} = 34 \Rightarrow x = 72$

11) $4(x - 12) = 40 \Rightarrow x = 22$

12) $\frac{5x - 20}{6} = 80 \Rightarrow x = 100$

13) $3x - 15 = -6 \Rightarrow x = 3$

14) $3x - 15 = 3 \Rightarrow x = 6$

15) $\frac{5x - 20}{6} = 60 \Rightarrow x = 76$

16) $3x - 6 = 12 \Rightarrow x = 6$

17) $\frac{5x - 25}{2} = 40 \Rightarrow x = 21$

18) $3x - 9 = -15 \Rightarrow x = -2$

19) $\frac{3x - 12}{4} = 42 \Rightarrow x = 60$

20) $\frac{2x - 6}{5} = 14 \Rightarrow x = 38$

21) $\frac{3x - 6}{3} = 12 \Rightarrow x = 14$

22) $3x - 6 = 27 \Rightarrow x = 11$

Multi Step Equations

Solve each equation.

1) $\frac{2x - 15}{7} = 48 - \frac{1}{7}x$

2) $5x - 28 = 140 - 2x$

3) $2x - 8 + 3x = 52 + x$

4) $\frac{6x - 14}{4} = 133 - \frac{1}{4}x$

5) $5x - 28 = 119 - 2x$

6) $7x - 27 = 99 - 2x$

7) $3x - 20 + 3x = 100 + x$

8) $7x - 18 + 3x = 90 + x$

9) $6x - 16 + 3x = 40 + x$

10) $3x - 20 + 3x = 35 + x$

11) $4x - 18 = 60 - 2x$

12) $7x - 18 = 117 - 2x$

13) $\frac{5x - 24}{5} = 6 - \frac{1}{5}x$

14) $4x - 30 = 12 - 2x$

15) $5x - 14 = 21 - 2x$

16) $\frac{5x - 12}{7} = 24 - \frac{1}{7}x$

17) $\frac{6x - 21}{5} = 70 - \frac{1}{5}x$

18) $\frac{1x - 10}{3} = 6 - \frac{1}{3}x$

19) $6x - 40 = 128 - 2x$

20) $\frac{3x - 16}{7} = 32 - \frac{1}{7}x$

21) $5x - 21 = 56 - 2x$

22) $5x - 21 = 49 - 2x$

Answers of Multi Step Equations

✏️ **Solve each equation.**

1) $\frac{2x-15}{7} = 48 - \frac{1}{7}x \Rightarrow x = 117$

2) $5x - 28 = 140 - 2x \Rightarrow x = 24$

3) $2x - 8 + 3x = 52 + x \Rightarrow x = 15$

4) $\frac{6x-14}{4} = 133 - \frac{1}{4}x \Rightarrow x = 78$

5) $5x - 28 = 119 - 2x \Rightarrow x = 21$

6) $7x - 27 = 99 - 2x \Rightarrow x = 14$

7) $3x - 20 + 3x = 100 + x \Rightarrow x = 24$

8) $7x - 18 + 3x = 90 + x \Rightarrow x = 12$

9) $6x - 16 + 3x = 40 + x \Rightarrow x = 7$

10) $3x - 20 + 3x = 35 + x \Rightarrow x = 11$

11) $4x - 18 = 60 - 2x \Rightarrow x = 13$

12) $7x - 18 = 117 - 2x \Rightarrow x = 15$

13) $\frac{5x-24}{5} = 6 - \frac{1}{5}x \Rightarrow x = 9$

14) $4x - 30 = 12 - 2x \Rightarrow x = 7$

15) $5x - 14 = 21 - 2x \Rightarrow x = 5$

16) $\frac{5x-12}{7} = 24 - \frac{1}{7}x \Rightarrow x = 30$

17) $\frac{6x-21}{5} = 70 - \frac{1}{5}x \Rightarrow x = 53$

18) $\frac{1x-10}{3} = 6 - \frac{1}{3}x \Rightarrow x = 14$

19) $6x - 40 = 128 - 2x \Rightarrow x = 21$

20) $\frac{3x-16}{7} = 32 - \frac{1}{7}x \Rightarrow x = 60$

21) $5x - 21 = 56 - 2x \Rightarrow x = 11$

22) $5x - 21 = 49 - 2x \Rightarrow x = 10$

Systems of Equations

✏️ Solve each system of equations.

1) $3x + 7y = 34$
$3x + 2y = 14$
$x = \underline{}\quad y = \underline{}$

2) $2x + 6y = -10$
$4x + 2y = 10$
$x = \underline{}\quad y = \underline{}$

3) $5x + 2y = -3$
$7x + 7y = 0$
$x = \underline{}\quad y = \underline{}$

4) $4x + 7y = -8$
$4x + 2y = 12$
$x = \underline{}\quad y = \underline{}$

5) $4x + 5y = 24$
$2x + 4y = 18$
$x = \underline{}\quad y = \underline{}$

6) $5x + 7y = -41$
$5x + 5y = -35$
$x = \underline{}\quad y = \underline{}$

7) $4x + 2y = -20$
$5x + 4y = -28$
$x = \underline{}\quad y = \underline{}$

8) $2x + 2y = 4$
$4x + 4y = 8$
$x = \underline{}\quad y = \underline{}$

9) $2x + 6y = -6$
$7x + 6y = 9$
$x = \underline{}\quad y = \underline{}$

10) $4x + 3y = -2$
$7x + 3y = -8$
$x = \underline{}\quad y = \underline{}$

11) $2x + 5y = 30$
$7x + 7y = 63$
$x = \underline{}\quad y = \underline{}$

12) $4x + 4y = 0$
$3x + 7y = -16$
$x = \underline{}\quad y = \underline{}$

13) $4x + 4y = 20$
$2x + 6y = 30$
$x = \underline{}\quad y = \underline{}$

14) $4x + 3y = -18$
$3x + 2y = -13$
$x = \underline{}\quad y = \underline{}$

15) $4x + 3y = 1$
$4x + 2y = 2$
$x = \underline{}\quad y = \underline{}$

16) $5x + 3y = 10$
$5x + 5y = 20$
$x = \underline{}\quad y = \underline{}$

Answers of Systems of Equations

✏️ **Solve each system of equations.**

1) $3x + 7y = 34$
   $3x + 2y = 14$
   ─────────────
   $x = 2 \quad y = 4$

2) $2x + 6y = -10$
   $4x + 2y = 10$
   ─────────────
   $x = 4 \quad y = -3$

3) $5x + 2y = -3$
   $7x + 7y = 0$
   ─────────────
   $x = -1 \quad y = 1$

4) $4x + 7y = -8$
   $4x + 2y = 12$
   ─────────────
   $x = 5 \quad y = -4$

5) $4x + 5y = 24$
   $2x + 4y = 18$
   ─────────────
   $x = 1 \quad y = 4$

6) $5x + 7y = -41$
   $5x + 5y = -35$
   ─────────────
   $x = -4 \quad y = -3$

7) $4x + 2y = -20$
   $5x + 4y = -28$
   ─────────────
   $x = -4 \quad y = -2$

8) $2x + 2y = 4$
   $4x + 4y = 8$
   ─────────────
   $x = -2 \quad y = 4$

9) $2x + 6y = -6$
   $7x + 6y = 9$
   ─────────────
   $x = 3 \quad y = -2$

10) $4x + 3y = -2$
    $7x + 3y = -8$
    ─────────────
    $x = -2 \quad y = 2$

11) $2x + 5y = 30$
    $7x + 7y = 63$
    ─────────────
    $x = 5 \quad y = 4$

12) $4x + 4y = 0$
    $3x + 7y = -16$
    ─────────────
    $x = 4 \quad y = -4$

13) $4x + 4y = 20$
    $2x + 6y = 30$
    ─────────────
    $x = 0 \quad y = 5$

14) $4x + 3y = -18$
    $3x + 2y = -13$
    ─────────────
    $x = -3 \quad y = -2$

15) $4x + 3y = 1$
    $4x + 2y = 2$
    ─────────────
    $x = 1 \quad y = -1$

16) $5x + 3y = 10$
    $5x + 5y = 20$
    ─────────────
    $x = -1 \quad y = 5$

Systems of Equations Word Problems

 Solve each word problem.

1) At a store, Eva bought 5 shirts and 5 hats for $45. Nicole bought 7 same shirts and 6 same hats for $59. What is the price of each shirt?

2) A theater is selling tickets for a performance. Mr. Smith purchased 5 senior tickets and 7 child tickets for $58 for his friends and family. Mr. Jackson purchased 7 senior tickets and 6 child tickets for $66. What is the price of a senior ticket?

3) Emma and Sepehr are selling Chocolate Chip cookies and Oreo cookies Emma sold 6 boxes of Chocolate Chip cookies and 3 boxes of Oreo cookies for a total of $48. Sepehr sold 2 boxes of Chocolate Chip cookies and 2 boxes of Oreo cookies for a total of $22. Find the cost of one box of Chocolate Chip cookies.

4) Emma and Sepehr are selling Chocolate Chip cookies and Oreo cookies Emma sold 2 boxes of Chocolate Chip cookies and 6 boxes of Oreo cookies for a total of $44. Sepehr sold 3 boxes of Chocolate Chip cookies and 2 boxes of Oreo cookies for a total of $24. Find the cost of one box of Chocolate Chip cookies.

5) Tickets to a movie cost $5 for adults and $4 for students. A group of friends purchased 12 tickets for $54. How many adults ticket did they buy?

6) Tickets to a movie cost $2 for adults and $2 for students. A group of friends purchased 10 tickets for $20. How many adults ticket did they buy?

7) At a store, Eva bought 3 shirts and 2 hats for $20. Nicole bought 7 same shirts and 2 same hats for $36. What is the price of each shirt?

8) A theater is selling tickets for a performance. Mr. Smith purchased 5 senior tickets and 6 child tickets for $50 for his friends and family. Mr. Jackson purchased 3 senior tickets and 5 child tickets for $37. What is the price of a senior ticket?

Answers of Systems of Equations Word Problems

✏️ **Solve each word problem.**

1) At a store, Eva bought 5 shirts and 5 hats for $45. Nicole bought 7 same shirts and 6 same hats for $59. What is the price of each shirt? $5

2) A theater is selling tickets for a performance. Mr. Smith purchased 5 senior tickets and 7 child tickets for $58 for his friends and family. Mr. Jackson purchased 7 senior tickets and 6 child tickets for $66. What is the price of a senior ticket? $6

3) Emma and Sepehr are selling Chocolate Chip cookies and Oreo cookies Emma sold 6 boxes of Chocolate Chip cookies and 3 boxes of Oreo cookies for a total of $48. Sepehr sold 2 boxes of Chocolate Chip cookies and 2 boxes of Oreo cookies for a total of $22. Find the cost of one box of Chocolate Chip cookies. 5

4) Emma and Sepehr are selling Chocolate Chip cookies and Oreo cookies Emma sold 2 boxes of Chocolate Chip cookies and 6 boxes of Oreo cookies for a total of $44. Sepehr sold 3 boxes of Chocolate Chip cookies and 2 boxes of Oreo cookies for a total of $24. Find the cost of one box of Chocolate Chip cookies. 4

5) Tickets to a movie cost $5 for adults and $4 for students. A group of friends purchased 12 tickets for $54. How many adults ticket did they buy? 6 tickets.

6) Tickets to a movie cost $2 for adults and $2 for students. A group of friends purchased 10 tickets for $20. How many adults ticket did they buy? 6 tickets.

7) At a store, Eva bought 3 shirts and 2 hats for $20. Nicole bought 7 same shirts and 2 same hats for $36. What is the price of each shirt? $4

8) A theater is selling tickets for a performance. Mr. Smith purchased 5 senior tickets and 6 child tickets for $50 for his friends and family. Mr. Jackson purchased 3 senior tickets and 5 child tickets for $37. What is the price of a senior ticket? $4

Quadratic Equations

✏️ **Multiply.**

1) $(x+5)(x+4) =$

2) $(x+8)(x+1) =$

3) $(x+2)(x-2) =$

4) $(x+1)(x+4) =$

5) $(x+1)(x+2) =$

6) $(x+2)(x+5) =$

7) $(x-5)(x-1) =$

8) $(x+3)(x+5) =$

9) $(x-5)(x+3) =$

10) $(x-1)(x+3) =$

11) $(x-5)(x+5) =$

12) $(x-5)(x-2) =$

13) $(x+5)(x-2) =$

14) $(x-1)(x-3) =$

15) $(x-1)(x+5) =$

16) $(x-4)(x+8) =$

17) $(x+3)(x+2) =$

18) $(x-2)(x-4) =$

19) $(x+2)(x+4) =$

20) $(x+8)(x+3) =$

21) $(x+1)(x-5) =$

22) $(x+3)(x-2) =$

Answers of Quadratic Equations

Multiply.

1) $(x + 5)(x + 4) = x^2 + 9x + 20$
2) $(x + 8)(x + 1) = x^2 + 9x + 8$
3) $(x + 2)(x - 2) = x^2 + 0x - 4$
4) $(x + 1)(x + 4) = x^2 + 5x + 4$
5) $(x + 1)(x + 2) = x^2 + 3x + 2$
6) $(x + 2)(x + 5) = x^2 + 7x + 10$
7) $(x - 5)(x - 1) = x^2 - 6x + 5$
8) $(x + 3)(x + 5) = x^2 + 8x + 15$
9) $(x - 5)(x + 3) = x^2 - 2x - 15$
10) $(x - 1)(x + 3) = x^2 + 2x - 3$
11) $(x - 5)(x + 5) = x^2 + 0x - 25$
12) $(x - 5)(x - 2) = x^2 - 7x + 10$
13) $(x + 5)(x - 2) = x^2 + 3x - 10$
14) $(x - 1)(x - 3) = x^2 - 4x + 3$
15) $(x - 1)(x + 5) = x^2 + 4x - 5$
16) $(x - 4)(x + 8) = x^2 + 4x - 32$
17) $(x + 3)(x + 2) = x^2 + 5x + 6$
18) $(x - 2)(x - 4) = x^2 - 6x + 8$
19) $(x + 2)(x + 4) = x^2 + 6x + 8$
20) $(x + 8)(x + 3) = x^2 + 11x + 24$
21) $(x + 1)(x - 5) = x^2 - 4x - 5$
22) $(x + 3)(x - 2) = x^2 + 1x - 6$

Graphing Single Variable Inequalities

✏️ **Graph each inequality.**

1) $6 \leq x$

2) $-10 \leq x$

3) $-4 \leq x$

4) $-2 \geq x$

5) $-3 < x$

6) $9 \geq x$

7) $8 > x$

8) $7 \leq x$

9) $-1 > x$

10) $-9 > x$

11) $7 \geq x$

12) $1 > x$

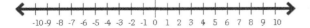

13) $-6 < x$

14) $-9 < x$

Answers of Graphing Single Variable Inequalities

 Graph each inequality.

1) $6 \leqslant x$

2) $-10 \leqslant x$

3) $-4 \leqslant x$

4) $-2 \geqslant x$

5) $-3 < x$

6) $9 \geqslant x$

7) $8 > x$

8) $7 \leqslant x$

9) $-1 > x$

10) $-9 > x$

11) $7 \geqslant x$

12) $1 > x$

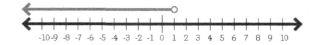

13) $-6 < x$

14) $-9 < x$

One Step Inequalities

Draw a graph for each inequality.

1) $8 < 8 + x$

2) $3 \leq 2 + x$

3) $7 + x \leq 4$

4) $6x \leq 30$

5) $15x > 30$

6) $4x \leq 32$

7) $8 + x \leq 2$

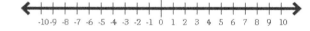

8) $10x \geq 50$

9) $14x < 56$

10) $8x \geq 8$

11) $3x < 18$

12) $11x \geq 33$

13) $14x > 56$

14) $9x \leq 45$

Answers of One Step Inequalities

✏️ **Draw a graph for each inequality.**

1) $8 < 8 + x$
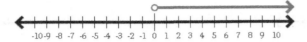

2) $3 \leqslant 2 + x$

3) $7 + x \leqslant 4$

4) $6x \leqslant 30$

5) $15x > 30$

6) $4x \leqslant 32$

7) $8 + x \leqslant 2$

8) $10x \geqslant 50$

9) $14x < 56$

10) $8x \geqslant 8$

11) $3x < 18$

12) $11x \geqslant 33$

13) $14x > 56$

14) $9x \leqslant 45$

Two Step Inequalities

✏️ **Draw a graph for each inequality.**

1) $-5x + 6 \leq -34$

2) $-3x + 19 > 4$

3) $-3x + 10 > -2$

4) $-6x + 7 \geq -11$

5) $-4x + 7 < 3$

6) $7x + 7 \geq 35$

7) $3x + 13 \leq 25$

8) $-9x + 5 < -22$

9) $-8x + 17 \leq 9$

10) $-5x + 3 \geq -2$

11) $8x + 19 \geq 51$

12) $-9x + 18 \leq -18$

13) $6x + 9 \leq 45$

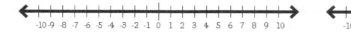

14) $-7x + 7 > -42$

Answers of Two Step Inequalities

 Draw a graph for each inequality.

1) $-5x + 6 \leq -34$

2) $-3x + 19 > 4$

3) $-3x + 10 > -2$

4) $-6x + 7 \geq -11$

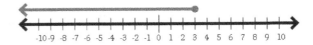

5) $-4x + 7 < 3$

6) $7x + 7 \geq 35$

7) $3x + 13 \leq 25$

8) $-9x + 5 < -22$

9) $-8x + 17 \leq 9$

10) $-5x + 3 \geq -2$

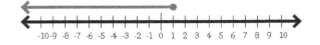

11) $8x + 19 \geq 51$

12) $-9x + 18 \leq -18$

13) $6x + 9 \leq 45$

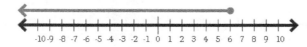

14) $-7x + 7 > -42$

Multi Step Inequalities

✏️ **Draw a graph for each inequality.**

1) $8(x+11) < 136$

2) $4(x+2) \leq 32$

3) $2(x+19) < 42$

4) $3(x+6) \leq 39$

5) $4(x+9) < 40$

6) $2(x+1) \geq 10$

7) $\frac{x-32}{4} \geq -8$

8) $\frac{x-24}{3} \geq -8$

9) $6(x+2) \geq 54$

10) $\frac{x-6}{3} \geq -2$

11) $2(x+3) \geq 20$

12) $5(x+4) < 25$

13) $\frac{x-18}{2} \geq -7$

14) $7(x+15) \geq 126$

Answers of Multi Step Inequalities

✏️ **Draw a graph for each inequality.**

1) $8(x+11) < 136$
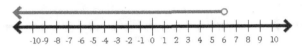

2) $4(x+2) \leqslant 32$

3) $2(x+19) < 42$

4) $3(x+6) \leqslant 39$

5) $4(x+9) < 40$
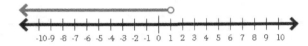

6) $2(x+1) \geqslant 10$

7) $\frac{x-32}{4} \geqslant -8$

8) $\frac{x-24}{3} \geqslant -8$

9) $6(x+2) \geqslant 54$

10) $\frac{x-6}{3} \geqslant -2$
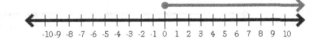

11) $2(x+3) \geqslant 20$

12) $5(x+4) < 25$
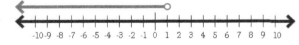

13) $\frac{x-18}{2} \geqslant -7$

14) $7(x+15) \geqslant 126$

Multiplication Property of Exponents

Simplify.

1) $5x^2 \times 4yx^4 =$

2) $8x^7 \times x^5 \times x =$

3) $3x^2 \times 4yx^3 =$

4) $5y^4x^2 \times 3y^3x^4 =$

5) $4^3 \times 4 =$

6) $3y^7x^4 \times 4y^3x^4 =$

7) $5x^4 \times x^6 \times x =$

8) $(2x^3)^2 =$

9) $8y^7x^2 \times 3y^4x^3 =$

10) $6^6 \times 6 =$

11) $(10x^3)^2 =$

12) $8^4 \times 8^6 =$

13) $10^5 \times 10 =$

14) $3x^2 \times x^3 \times x =$

15) $9y^2x^4 \times 4y^2x^4 =$

16) $(8x^6)^2 =$

17) $2x^2 \times 3yx^6 =$

18) $11^7 \times 11^4 =$

19) $3^7 \times 3 =$

20) $8^3 \times 8 =$

21) $9x^4 \times 3yx^5 =$

22) $8x^5 \times 2yx^4 =$

Answers of Multiplication Property of Exponents

✏️ **Simplify.**

1) $5x^2 \times 4yx^4 = 20yx^6$

2) $8x^7 \times x^5 \times x = 8x^{13}$

3) $3x^2 \times 4yx^3 = 12yx^5$

4) $5y^4x^2 \times 3y^3x^4 = 15y^7x^6$

5) $4^3 \times 4 = 4^4$

6) $3y^7x^4 \times 4y^3x^4 = 12y^{10}x^8$

7) $5x^4 \times x^6 \times x = 5x^{11}$

8) $(2x^3)^2 = 4x^6$

9) $8y^7x^2 \times 3y^4x^3 = 24y^{11}x^5$

10) $6^6 \times 6 = 6^7$

11) $(10x^3)^2 = 100x^6$

12) $8^4 \times 8^6 = 8^{10}$

13) $10^5 \times 10 = 10^6$

14) $3x^2 \times x^3 \times x = 3x^6$

15) $9y^2x^4 \times 4y^2x^4 = 36y^4x^8$

16) $(8x^6)^2 = 64x^{12}$

17) $2x^2 \times 3yx^6 = 6yx^8$

18) $11^7 \times 11^4 = 11^{11}$

19) $3^7 \times 3 = 3^8$

20) $8^3 \times 8 = 8^4$

21) $9x^4 \times 3yx^5 = 27yx^9$

22) $8x^5 \times 2yx^4 = 16yx^9$

Division Property of Exponents

Simplify.

1) $\dfrac{20x^{-6}}{2x^{-3}y^2} =$

2) $\dfrac{12x^{-6}}{4x^{-4}y^4} =$

3) $\dfrac{6x^6}{2x^3} =$

4) $\dfrac{24x^{-7}}{3x^{-3}} =$

5) $\dfrac{33x^{-8}}{3x^{-4}} =$

6) $\dfrac{18x^{-6}}{2x^{-2}} =$

7) $\dfrac{7^6}{7} =$

8) $\dfrac{18x^{-7}}{3x^{-4}y^3} =$

9) $\dfrac{8x^{-7}}{2x^{-3}} =$

10) $\dfrac{10x^{-8}}{2x^{-3}y^2} =$

11) $\dfrac{14x^{-8}}{2x^{-4}} =$

12) $\dfrac{16x^6}{4x^3} =$

13) $\dfrac{21x^7}{3x^3} =$

14) $\dfrac{12x^{-7}}{3x^{-4}y^3} =$

15) $\dfrac{20x^{-8}}{4x^{-3}} =$

16) $\dfrac{2^6}{2} =$

17) $\dfrac{6^7}{6} =$

18) $\dfrac{11^6}{11} =$

19) $\dfrac{10^3}{10} =$

20) $\dfrac{20x^8}{2x^4} =$

21) $\dfrac{18x^7}{3x^2} =$

22) $\dfrac{16x^7}{2x^2} =$

Answers of Division Property of Exponents

✏️ **Simplify.**

1) $\dfrac{20x^{-6}}{2x^{-3}y^2} = \dfrac{10}{x^3 y^2}$

2) $\dfrac{12x^{-6}}{4x^{-4}y^4} = \dfrac{3}{x^2 y^4}$

3) $\dfrac{6x^6}{2x^3} = 3x^3$

4) $\dfrac{24x^{-7}}{3x^{-3}} = \dfrac{8}{x^4}$

5) $\dfrac{33x^{-8}}{3x^{-4}} = \dfrac{11}{x^4}$

6) $\dfrac{18x^{-6}}{2x^{-2}} = \dfrac{9}{x^4}$

7) $\dfrac{7^6}{7} = 7^5$

8) $\dfrac{18x^{-7}}{3x^{-4}y^3} = \dfrac{6}{x^3 y^3}$

9) $\dfrac{8x^{-7}}{2x^{-3}} = \dfrac{4}{x^4}$

10) $\dfrac{10x^{-8}}{2x^{-3}y^2} = \dfrac{5}{x^5 y^2}$

11) $\dfrac{14x^{-8}}{2x^{-4}} = \dfrac{7}{x^4}$

12) $\dfrac{16x^6}{4x^3} = 4x^3$

13) $\dfrac{21x^7}{3x^3} = 7x^4$

14) $\dfrac{12x^{-7}}{3x^{-4}y^3} = \dfrac{4}{x^3 y^3}$

15) $\dfrac{20x^{-8}}{4x^{-3}} = \dfrac{5}{x^5}$

16) $\dfrac{2^6}{2} = 2^5$

17) $\dfrac{6^7}{6} = 6^6$

18) $\dfrac{11^6}{11} = 11^5$

19) $\dfrac{10^3}{10} = 10^2$

20) $\dfrac{20x^8}{2x^4} = 10x^4$

21) $\dfrac{18x^7}{3x^2} = 6x^5$

22) $\dfrac{16x^7}{2x^2} = 8x^5$

Powers of Products and Quotients

✏️ Simplify.

1) $(-2x^4)^2 =$

2) $(-x^4 x^2)^2 =$

3) $(9x^2 y)^3 =$

4) $(-3x^3 y)^2 =$

5) $(x^3 y)^2 =$

6) $(-x^3)^2 =$

7) $(-6x^3 y)^2 =$

8) $(5x^2 y)^3 =$

9) $(-2x^4 y)^2 =$

10) $(-10x^4 y)^3 =$

11) $(-3x^2 x^2)^3 =$

12) $(7x^3)^3 =$

13) $(x^4)^2 =$

14) $(-9x^2)^3 =$

15) $(8x^3 y)^2 =$

16) $(3x^4 x^2)^2 =$

17) $(2x^2 x^2)^3 =$

18) $(-10x^4)^2 =$

19) $(8x^4 x^2)^3 =$

20) $(x^4 x^2)^2 =$

21) $(3x^4 y)^3 =$

22) $(-7x^2 y)^2 =$

Answers of Powers of Products and Quotients

✏️ **Simplify.**

1) $(-2x^4)^2 = 4x^8$

2) $(-x^4x^2)^2 = 1x^{12}$

3) $(9x^2y)^3 = 729x^6y^3$

4) $(-3x^3y)^2 = 9x^6y^2$

5) $(x^3y)^2 = 1x^6y^2$

6) $(-x^3)^2 = 1x^6$

7) $(-6x^3y)^2 = 36x^6y^2$

8) $(5x^2y)^3 = 125x^6y^3$

9) $(-2x^4y)^2 = 4x^8y^2$

10) $(-10x^4y)^3 = -1000x^{12}y^3$

11) $(-3x^2x^2)^3 = -27x^{12}$

12) $(7x^3)^3 = 343x^9$

13) $(x^4)^2 = 1x^8$

14) $(-9x^2)^3 = -729x^6$

15) $(8x^3y)^2 = 64x^6y^2$

16) $(3x^4x^2)^2 = 9x^{12}$

17) $(2x^2x^2)^3 = 8x^{12}$

18) $(-10x^4)^2 = 100x^8$

19) $(8x^4x^2)^3 = 512x^{18}$

20) $(x^4x^2)^2 = 1x^{12}$

21) $(3x^4y)^3 = 27x^{12}y^3$

22) $(-7x^2y)^2 = 49x^4y^2$

Zero and Negative Exponents

▶ **Evaluate the following expressions.**

1) $9^{-4} =$

2) $2^{-2} =$

3) $0^4 =$

4) $10^{-2} =$

5) $4^{-5} =$

6) $0^6 =$

7) $0^5 =$

8) $10^{-5} =$

9) $-5^{-3} =$

10) $0^3 =$

11) $-7^{-2} =$

12) $8^{-2} =$

13) $5^{-3} =$

14) $12^{-4} =$

15) $-3^{-5} =$

16) $7^{-3} =$

17) $0^2 =$

18) $-12^{-4} =$

19) $0^7 =$

20) $10^{-4} =$

21) $10^{-3} =$

22) $-9^{-3} =$

Answers of Zero and Negative Exponents

✏️ **Evaluate the following expressions.**

1) $9^{-4} = \frac{1}{9^4}$

2) $2^{-2} = \frac{1}{2^2}$

3) $0^4 = 0$

4) $10^{-2} = \frac{1}{100}$

5) $4^{-5} = \frac{1}{4^5}$

6) $0^6 = 0$

7) $0^5 = 0$

8) $10^{-5} = \frac{1}{100000}$

9) $-5^{-3} = \frac{1}{-5^3}$

10) $0^3 = 0$

11) $-7^{-2} = \frac{1}{-7^2}$

12) $8^{-2} = \frac{1}{8^2}$

13) $5^{-3} = \frac{1}{5^3}$

14) $12^{-4} = \frac{1}{12^4}$

15) $-3^{-5} = \frac{1}{-3^5}$

16) $7^{-3} = \frac{1}{7^3}$

17) $0^2 = 0$

18) $-12^{-4} = \frac{1}{-12^4}$

19) $0^7 = 0$

20) $10^{-4} = \frac{1}{10000}$

21) $10^{-3} = \frac{1}{1000}$

22) $-9^{-3} = \frac{1}{-9^3}$

Negative Exponents and Negative Bases

Simplify.

1) $\left(\dfrac{-7}{2}\right)^{-2} =$

2) $\dfrac{6x^3}{-2y^{-4}} =$

3) $-\dfrac{9x}{x^{-5}} =$

4) $-\dfrac{4x}{x^{-4}} =$

5) $\dfrac{3x^3}{-4y^{-2}} =$

6) $-\dfrac{2x}{x^{-2}} =$

7) $\dfrac{19x^3}{-2y^{-5}} =$

8) $-\dfrac{10x}{x^{-2}} =$

9) $-\dfrac{8}{x^{-3}} =$

10) $-\dfrac{21x}{x^{-4}} =$

11) $-\dfrac{3x}{x^{-4}} =$

12) $-\dfrac{16}{x^{-4}} =$

13) $-\dfrac{20}{x^{-3}} =$

14) $-\dfrac{11x}{x^{-3}} =$

15) $\left(\dfrac{4}{3}\right)^{-2} =$

16) $-\dfrac{10}{x^{-5}} =$

17) $-\dfrac{17}{x^{-3}} =$

18) $\left(\dfrac{12}{3}\right)^{-2} =$

19) $\left(\dfrac{3}{4}\right)^{-2} =$

20) $\left(\dfrac{-3}{3}\right)^{-2} =$

21) $-\dfrac{11}{x^{-3}} =$

22) $-\dfrac{19x}{x^{-3}} =$

Answers of Negative Exponents and Negative Bases

Simplify.

1) $\left(\frac{-7}{2}\right)^{-2} = \frac{4}{49}$

2) $\frac{6x^3}{-2y^{-4}} = -\frac{6x^3y^4}{2}$

3) $-\frac{9x}{x^{-5}} = -9x^6$

4) $-\frac{4x}{x^{-4}} = -4x^5$

5) $\frac{3x^3}{-4y^{-2}} = -\frac{3x^3y^2}{4}$

6) $-\frac{2x}{x^{-2}} = -2x^3$

7) $\frac{19x^3}{-2y^{-5}} = -\frac{19x^3y^5}{2}$

8) $-\frac{10x}{x^{-2}} = -10x^3$

9) $-\frac{8}{x^{-3}} = -8x^3$

10) $-\frac{21x}{x^{-4}} = -21x^5$

11) $-\frac{3x}{x^{-4}} = -3x^5$

12) $-\frac{16}{x^{-4}} = -16x^4$

13) $-\frac{20}{x^{-3}} = -20x^3$

14) $-\frac{11x}{x^{-3}} = -11x^4$

15) $\left(\frac{4}{3}\right)^{-2} = \frac{9}{16}$

16) $-\frac{10}{x^{-5}} = -10x^5$

17) $-\frac{17}{x^{-3}} = -17x^3$

18) $\left(\frac{12}{3}\right)^{-2} = \frac{9}{144}$

19) $\left(\frac{3}{4}\right)^{-2} = \frac{16}{9}$

20) $\left(\frac{-3}{3}\right)^{-2} = \frac{9}{9}$

21) $-\frac{11}{x^{-3}} = -11x^3$

22) $-\frac{19x}{x^{-3}} = -19x^4$

Square Roots

Solve.

1) $\sqrt{324} =$

2) $\sqrt{100} =$

3) $\sqrt{245} =$

4) $\sqrt{300} =$

5) $\sqrt{1} =$

6) $\sqrt{16} =$

7) $\sqrt{45} =$

8) $\sqrt{49} =$

9) $\sqrt{363} =$

10) $\sqrt{144} =$

11) $\sqrt{9} =$

12) $\sqrt{4} =$

13) $\sqrt{72} =$

14) $\sqrt{588} =$

15) $\sqrt{81} =$

16) $\sqrt{192} =$

17) $\sqrt{32} =$

18) $\sqrt{64} =$

19) $\sqrt{169} =$

20) $\sqrt{25} =$

21) $\sqrt{121} =$

22) $\sqrt{100} =$

Answers of Square Roots

Solve.

1) $\sqrt{324} = 9\sqrt{4}$

2) $\sqrt{100} = 10$

3) $\sqrt{245} = 7\sqrt{5}$

4) $\sqrt{300} = 10\sqrt{3}$

5) $\sqrt{1} = 1$

6) $\sqrt{16} = 4$

7) $\sqrt{45} = 3\sqrt{5}$

8) $\sqrt{49} = 7$

9) $\sqrt{363} = 11\sqrt{3}$

10) $\sqrt{144} = 12$

11) $\sqrt{9} = 3$

12) $\sqrt{4} = 2$

13) $\sqrt{72} = 6\sqrt{2}$

14) $\sqrt{588} = 14\sqrt{3}$

15) $\sqrt{81} = 9$

16) $\sqrt{192} = 8\sqrt{3}$

17) $\sqrt{32} = 4\sqrt{2}$

18) $\sqrt{64} = 8$

19) $\sqrt{169} = 13$

20) $\sqrt{25} = 5$

21) $\sqrt{121} = 11$

22) $\sqrt{100} = 5\sqrt{4}$

Graphing Lines Using Slope Intercept Form

✏️ **Sketch the graph of each line.**

1) $y = -2x + 4$

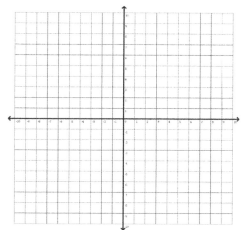

2) $y = x + 2$

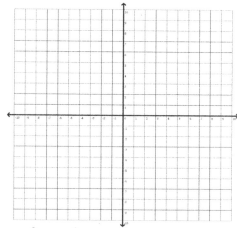

3) $y = -4x - 1$

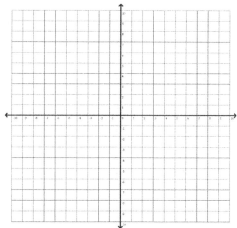

4) $y = 2x - 3$

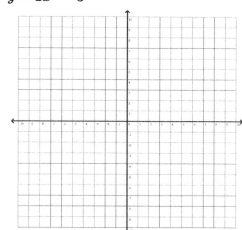

5) $y = 6x - 3$

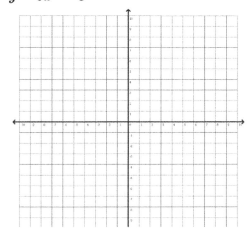

6) $y = -2x - 5$

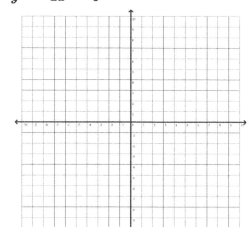

Answers of Graphing Lines Using Slope Intercept Form

Sketch the graph of each line.

1) $y = -2x + 4$

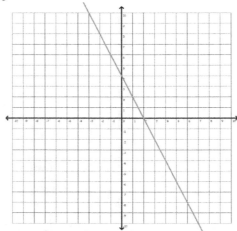

2) $y = x + 2$

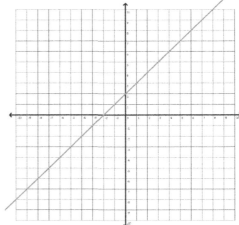

3) $y = -4x - 1$

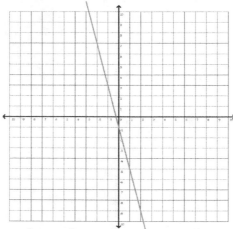

4) $y = 2x - 3$

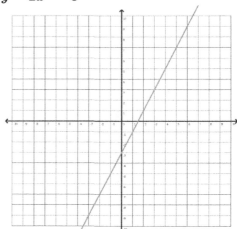

5) $y = 6x - 3$

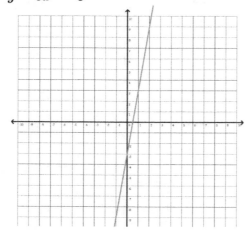

6) $y = -2x - 5$

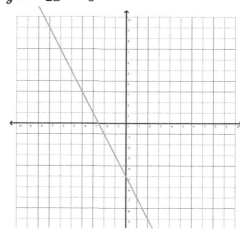

Graphing Lines Using Standard Form

✏️ **Sketch the graph of each line.**

1) $-24x + 4y - 16 = 0$

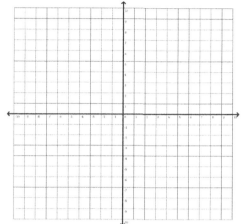

2) $-8x - 4y - 16 = 0$

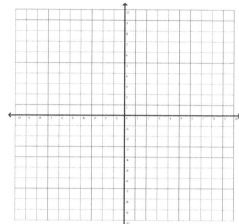

3) $4x - y - 2 = 0$

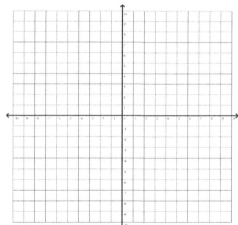

4) $-2x - y - 5 = 0$

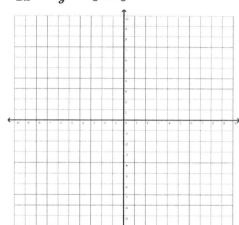

5) $6x - y - 4 = 0$

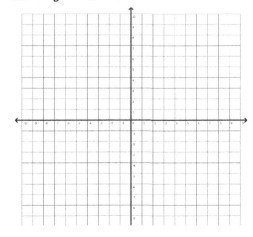

6) $3x - y - 2 = 0$

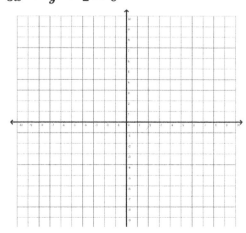

Answers of Graphing Lines Using Standard Form

Sketch the graph of each line.

1) $-24x + 4y - 16 = 0$

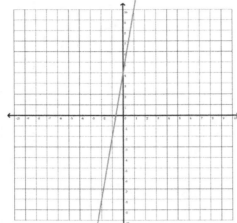

2) $-8x - 4y - 16 = 0$

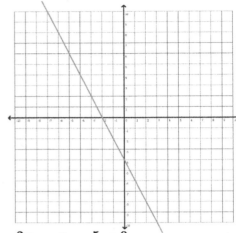

3) $4x - y - 2 = 0$

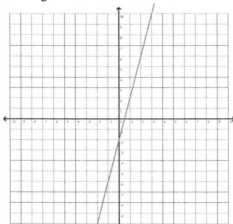

4) $-2x - y - 5 = 0$

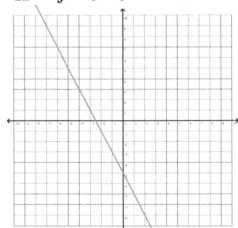

5) $6x - y - 4 = 0$

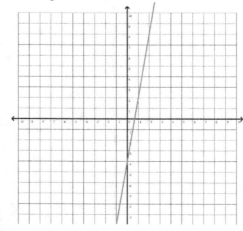

6) $3x - y - 2 = 0$

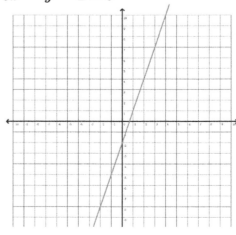

Writing Linear Equations

✏️ **Find the equation of the line passing through the given points.**

1) $(8, 1)(9, 1)$

2) $(5, 6)(6, 3)$

3) $(7, 1)(8, 5)$

4) $(6, 7)(7, -6)$

5) $(6, 4)(7, 0)$

6) $(9, 1)(10, 4)$

7) $(4, 8)(5, 0)$

8) $(2, 7)(3, -1)$

9) $(5, 3)(6, -2)$

10) $(8, 10)(9, -4)$

11) $(7, 8)(8, -1)$

12) $(7, 6)(8, -5)$

13) $(5, 2)(6, -1)$

14) $(10, 7)(11, -1)$

15) $(8, 9)(9, 1)$

16) $(1, 10)(2, -6)$

17) $(3, 4)(4, 1)$

18) $(7, 4)(8, -6)$

19) $(2, 4)(3, -3)$

20) $(10, 2)(11, 3)$

21) $(6, 6)(7, -4)$

22) $(3, 8)(4, 3)$

Answers of Writing Linear Equations

✏️ **Find the equation of the line passing through the given points.**

1) $(8,1)(9,1) \Rightarrow y = 0x + 1$

2) $(5,6)(6,3) \Rightarrow y = -3x + 21$

3) $(7,1)(8,5) \Rightarrow y = 4x - 27$

4) $(6,7)(7,-6) \Rightarrow y = -13x + 85$

5) $(6,4)(7,0) \Rightarrow y = -4x + 28$

6) $(9,1)(10,4) \Rightarrow y = 3x - 26$

7) $(4,8)(5,0) \Rightarrow y = -8x + 40$

8) $(2,7)(3,-1) \Rightarrow y = -8x + 23$

9) $(5,3)(6,-2) \Rightarrow y = -5x + 28$

10) $(8,10)(9,-4) \Rightarrow y = -14x + 122$

11) $(7,8)(8,-1) \Rightarrow y = -9x + 71$

12) $(7,6)(8,-5) \Rightarrow y = -11x + 83$

13) $(5,2)(6,-1) \Rightarrow y = -3x + 17$

14) $(10,7)(11,-1) \Rightarrow y = -8x + 87$

15) $(8,9)(9,1) \Rightarrow y = -8x + 73$

16) $(1,10)(2,-6) \Rightarrow y = -16x + 26$

17) $(3,4)(4,1) \Rightarrow y = -3x + 13$

18) $(7,4)(8,-6) \Rightarrow y = -10x + 74$

19) $(2,4)(3,-3) \Rightarrow y = -7x + 18$

20) $(10,2)(11,3) \Rightarrow y = x - 8$

21) $(6,6)(7,-4) \Rightarrow y = -10x + 66$

22) $(3,8)(4,3) \Rightarrow y = -5x + 23$

Graphing Linear Inequalities

✏️ **Sketch the graph of each linear inequality.**

1) $y < -5x + 1$

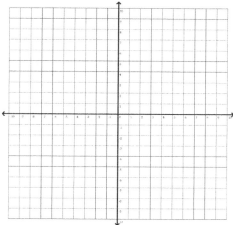

2) $y < 6x$

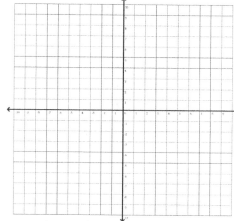

3) $y > x + 2$

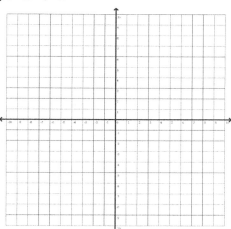

4) $y > -4x + 1$

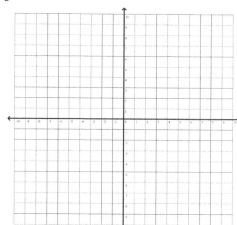

5) $y > 6x + 2$

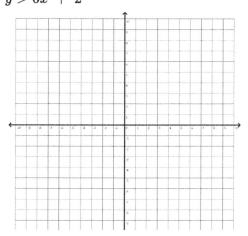

6) $y < x + 1$

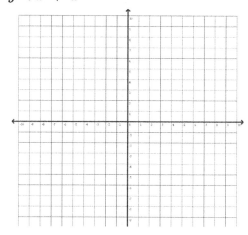

Answers of Graphing Linear Inequalities

✏️ **Sketch the graph of each linear inequality.**

1) $y < -5x + 1$

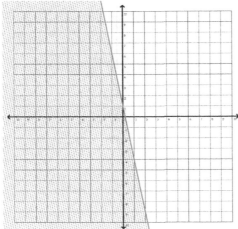

2) $y < 6x$

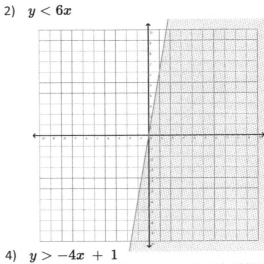

3) $y > x + 2$

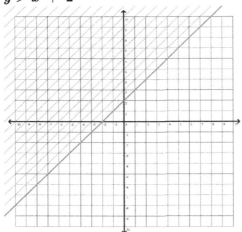

4) $y > -4x + 1$

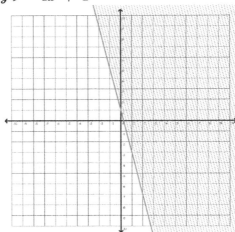

5) $y > 6x + 2$

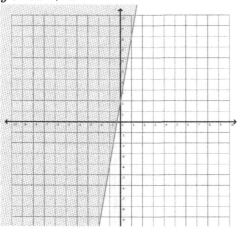

6) $y < x + 1$

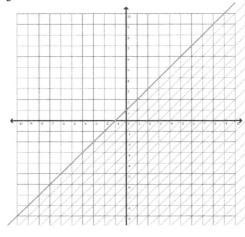

108

Finding Slope

✏️ **Find the slope of the line through each pair of points.**

1) $(2, 6), (3, 8)$

2) $(0, 5), (5, 55)$

3) $(2, 1), (1, 13)$

4) $(0, 0), (-3, 30)$

5) $(6, 1), (5, 15)$

6) $(2, 2), (1, -7)$

7) $(3, 3), (8, -77)$

8) $(6, 6), (11, 41)$

9) $(6, 2), (9, 65)$

10) $(6, 0), (3, 21)$

11) $(4, 4), (2, 44)$

12) $(3, 3), (-1, 79)$

13) $(3, 3), (2, -2)$

14) $(5, 0), (8, -33)$

15) $(5, 4), (7, -4)$

16) $(5, 5), (1, 29)$

17) $(5, 3), (4, -11)$

18) $(2, 0), (1, 17)$

19) $(1, 3), (0, -14)$

20) $(1, 1), (0, 6)$

21) $(2, 7), (5, 43)$

22) $(4, 1), (3, 4)$

Answers of Finding Slope

Find the slope of the line through each pair of points.

1) $(2, 6), (3, 8) \Rightarrow 2$

2) $(0, 5), (5, 55) \Rightarrow 10$

3) $(2, 1), (1, 13) \Rightarrow -12$

4) $(0, 0), (-3, 30) \Rightarrow -10$

5) $(6, 1), (5, 15) \Rightarrow -14$

6) $(2, 2), (1, -7) \Rightarrow 9$

7) $(3, 3), (8, -77) \Rightarrow -16$

8) $(6, 6), (11, 41) \Rightarrow 7$

9) $(6, 2), (9, 65) \Rightarrow 21$

10) $(6, 0), (3, 21) \Rightarrow -7$

11) $(4, 4), (2, 44) \Rightarrow -20$

12) $(3, 3), (-1, 79) \Rightarrow -19$

13) $(3, 3), (2, -2) \Rightarrow 5$

14) $(5, 0), (8, -33) \Rightarrow -11$

15) $(5, 4), (7, -4) \Rightarrow -4$

16) $(5, 5), (1, 29) \Rightarrow -6$

17) $(5, 3), (4, -11) \Rightarrow 14$

18) $(2, 0), (1, 17) \Rightarrow -17$

19) $(1, 3), (0, -14) \Rightarrow 17$

20) $(1, 1), (0, 6) \Rightarrow -5$

21) $(2, 7), (5, 43) \Rightarrow 12$

22) $(4, 1), (3, 4) \Rightarrow -3$

Finding Midpoint

✏️ **Find the midpoint of the line segment with the given endpoints.**

1) $(1, 2), (-7, -6)$

2) $(-8, -2), (4, -4)$

3) $(-6, 10), (4, -8)$

4) $(-4, 10), (2, -4)$

5) $(11, 1), (-7, 1)$

6) $(-6, -1), (4, -3)$

7) $(-5, 0), (5, 4)$

8) $(0, -10), (-4, 6)$

9) $(-13, 7), (7, -5)$

10) $(6, 2), (-8, -2)$

11) $(-3, -5), (1, 3)$

12) $(-9, 5), (3, 1)$

13) $(7, -6), (-7, 4)$

14) $(3, 1), (1, -5)$

15) $(-3, -5), (5, 3)$

16) $(-1, 9), (7, -7)$

17) $(6, -8), (0, 4)$

18) $(5, -1), (-1, -5)$

19) $(3, -3), (3, 7)$

20) $(-4, -3), (6, 7)$

21) $(-4, -5), (-2, 5)$

22) $(-5, -3), (5, -1)$

Answers of Finding Midpoint

✏️ **Find the midpoint of the line segment with the given endpoints.**

1) $(1, 2), (-7, -6) \Rightarrow M = (-3, -2)$
2) $(-8, -2), (4, -4) \Rightarrow M = (-2, -3)$

3) $(-6, 10), (4, -8) \Rightarrow M = (-1, 1)$
4) $(-4, 10), (2, -4) \Rightarrow M = (-1, 3)$

5) $(11, 1), (-7, 1) \Rightarrow M = (2, 1)$
6) $(-6, -1), (4, -3) \Rightarrow M = (-1, -2)$

7) $(-5, 0), (5, 4) \Rightarrow M = (0, 2)$
8) $(0, -10), (-4, 6) \Rightarrow M = (-2, -2)$

9) $(-13, 7), (7, -5) \Rightarrow M = (-3, 1)$
10) $(6, 2), (-8, -2) \Rightarrow M = (-1, 0)$

11) $(-3, -5), (1, 3) \Rightarrow M = (-1, -1)$
12) $(-9, 5), (3, 1) \Rightarrow M = (-3, 3)$

13) $(7, -6), (-7, 4) \Rightarrow M = (0, -1)$
14) $(3, 1), (1, -5) \Rightarrow M = (2, -2)$

15) $(-3, -5), (5, 3) \Rightarrow M = (1, -1)$
16) $(-1, 9), (7, -7) \Rightarrow M = (3, 1)$

17) $(6, -8), (0, 4) \Rightarrow M = (3, -2)$
18) $(5, -1), (-1, -5) \Rightarrow M = (2, -3)$

19) $(3, -3), (3, 7) \Rightarrow M = (3, 2)$
20) $(-4, -3), (6, 7) \Rightarrow M = (1, 2)$

21) $(-4, -5), (-2, 5) \Rightarrow M = (-3, 0)$
22) $(-5, -3), (5, -1) \Rightarrow M = (0, -2)$

Finding Distance of Two Points

✏️ **Find the distance between each pair of points.**

1) $(-4, -3), (4, -6)$

2) $(6, 2), (-6, 2)$

3) $(1, 2), (4, -2)$

4) $(0, -4), (7, 4)$

5) $(1, -6), (-6, 6)$

6) $(-3, 2), (1, -2)$

7) $(-2, -3), (2, -3)$

8) $(-4, -1), (4, 6)$

9) $(8, 4), (-4, -4)$

10) $(1, 1), (7, 5)$

11) $(-3, 9), (3, -1)$

12) $(8, -9), (-8, 1)$

13) $(5, 5), (-5, -2)$

14) $(-3, -6), (7, 6)$

15) $(7, 3), (-3, -3)$

16) $(-10, -4), (7, 4)$

17) $(3, -5), (-3, -5)$

18) $(-2, -7), (6, 7)$

19) $(1, -3), (-4, 3)$

20) $(7, 0), (-7, 4)$

21) $(4, -10), (-4, 5)$

22) $(-1, 1), (1, -4)$

Answers of Finding Distance of Two Points

✏️ **Find the distance between each pair of points.**

1) $(-4, -3), (4, -6) \Rightarrow D = 9$

2) $(6, 2), (-6, 2) \Rightarrow D = 4$

3) $(1, 2), (4, -2) \Rightarrow D = 5$

4) $(0, -4), (7, 4) \Rightarrow D = 7$

5) $(1, -6), (-6, 6) \Rightarrow D = 5$

6) $(-3, 2), (1, -2) \Rightarrow D = 2$

7) $(-2, -3), (2, -3) \Rightarrow D = 6$

8) $(-4, -1), (4, 6) \Rightarrow D = 5$

9) $(8, 4), (-4, -4) \Rightarrow D = 4$

10) $(1, 1), (7, 5) \Rightarrow D = 10$

11) $(-3, 9), (3, -1) \Rightarrow D = 8$

12) $(8, -9), (-8, 1) \Rightarrow D = 8$

13) $(5, 5), (-5, -2) \Rightarrow D = 3$

14) $(-3, -6), (7, 6) \Rightarrow D = 4$

15) $(7, 3), (-3, -3) \Rightarrow D = 4$

16) $(-10, -4), (7, 4) \Rightarrow D = 3$

17) $(3, -5), (-3, -5) \Rightarrow D = 10$

18) $(-2, -7), (6, 7) \Rightarrow D = 4$

19) $(1, -3), (-4, 3) \Rightarrow D = 3$

20) $(7, 0), (-7, 4) \Rightarrow D = 4$

21) $(4, -10), (-4, 5) \Rightarrow D = 5$

22) $(-1, 1), (1, -4) \Rightarrow D = 3$

Writing Polynomials in Standard Form

✏️ Write each polynomial in standard form.

1) $-6x^2 - x + 10x^3 =$

2) $-2(4x^3 - x) - 7x^4 =$

3) $-14x^2 - x + 18x^3 =$

4) $15x^2 - 16x^3 =$

5) $-13x^2 - 6 + 15x^3 =$

6) $x - 2(22x^3 - x) - 26x^4 =$

7) $-15x^2 - 5 + 18x^3 =$

8) $-2(19x^3 - x) - 23x^4 =$

9) $-22x^2 - x + 24x^3 =$

10) $8x^2 - 10x^3 =$

11) $-2(15x^3 - x) - 16x^4 =$

12) $-14x^2 - 6 + 17x^3 =$

13) $x - 2(8x^3 - x) - 12x^4 =$

Answers of Writing Polynomials in Standard Form

✏️ **Write each polynomial in standard form.**

1) $-6x^2 - x + 10x^3 = 10x^3 - 6x^2 - x$

2) $-2(4x^3 - x) - 7x^4 = -7x^4 - 8x^3 + 2x$

3) $-14x^2 - x + 18x^3 = 18x^3 - 14x^2 - x$

4) $15x^2 - 16x^3 = -16x^3 + 15x^2$

5) $-13x^2 - 6 + 15x^3 = 15x^3 - 13x^2 - 6$

6) $x - 2(22x^3 - x) - 26x^4 = -26x^4 - 44x^3 + 3x$

7) $-15x^2 - 5 + 18x^3 = 18x^3 - 15x^2 - 5$

8) $-2(19x^3 - x) - 23x^4 = -23x^4 - 38x^3 + 2x$

9) $-22x^2 - x + 24x^3 = 24x^3 - 22x^2 - x$

10) $8x^2 - 10x^3 = -10x^3 + 8x^2$

11) $-2(15x^3 - x) - 16x^4 = -16x^4 - 30x^3 + 2x$

12) $-14x^2 - 6 + 17x^3 = 17x^3 - 14x^2 - 6$

13) $x - 2(8x^3 - x) - 12x^4 = -12x^4 - 16x^3 + 3x$

Simplifying Polynomials

✏️ **Simplify each expression.**

1) $3x(x + 5x^2 - 2x^4) =$

2) $18 + 3(-2x^3 - 4x^2) - 2 + x =$

3) $13x(x + 2x^2 - 5x^4) =$

4) $20 + 5x^3 - 3x^2 - 2 =$

5) $(-x + 3x^2)x =$

6) $(-x + 21x^2)x =$

7) $(x - 12x^2)(x + 3) =$

8) $(x - 9x^2)(x + 3) =$

9) $2x(x + 7x^2 - 3x^4) =$

10) $11 + 3(-3x^3 - 2x^2) - 4 + x =$

11) $(-x + 11x^2)x =$

12) $19 + 3(-2x^3 - 2x^2) - 2 + x =$

13) $15x(x + 2x^2 - 7x^4) =$

Answers of Simplifying Polynomials

✏️ **Simplify each expression.**

1) $3x(x + 5x^2 - 2x^4) = -6x^4 + 15x^3 + 3x^2$

2) $18 + 3(-2x^3 - 4x^2) - 2 + x = -6x^3 - 12x^2 + x + 16$

3) $13x(x + 2x^2 - 5x^4) = -65x^4 + 26x^3 + 13x^2$

4) $20 + 5x^3 - 3x^2 - 2 = 5x^3 - 3x^2 + 18$

5) $(-x + 3x^2)x = 3x^3 - x^2$

6) $(-x + 21x^2)x = 21x^3 - x^2$

7) $(x - 12x^2)(x + 3) = -12x^3 - 35x^2 + 3x$

8) $(x - 9x^2)(x + 3) = -9x^3 - 26x^2 + 3x$

9) $2x(x + 7x^2 - 3x^4) = -6x^4 + 14x^3 + 2x^2$

10) $11 + 3(-3x^3 - 2x^2) - 4 + x = -9x^3 - 6x^2 + x + 7$

11) $(-x + 11x^2)x = 11x^3 - x^2$

12) $19 + 3(-2x^3 - 2x^2) - 2 + x = -6x^3 - 6x^2 + x + 17$

13) $15x(x + 2x^2 - 7x^4) = -105x^4 + 30x^3 + 15x^2$

Adding and Subtracting Polynomials

✏️ **Simplify each expression.**

1) $(-5x + 4) + (3x - 2) =$

2) $(-6x^2 + 7x) - (7x^2 + 5x) =$

3) $(9x + 6) - (4x + 4) =$

4) $(2x^2 + 7x) - (2x^2 + 3x) =$

5) $(7x^2 + 6x) + (3x^2 - 4x) =$

6) $(-8x + 6) + (4x - 4) =$

7) $(6x^2 + 3x) + (4x^2 - 2x) =$

8) $(9x^2 + 6x) - (7x^2 + 4x) =$

9) $(5x^2 + 8x) + (3x^2 - 6x) =$

10) $(-2x^2 + 7x) - (2x^2 + 5x) =$

11) $(-4x + 6) + (2x - 4) =$

12) $(-3x + 5) + (2x - 3) =$

13) $(5x^2 + 9x) - (3x^2 + 7x) =$

Answers of Adding and Subtracting Polynomials

✏️ **Simplify each expression.**

1) $(-5x + 4) + (3x - 2) = -2x + 2$

2) $(-6x^2 + 7x) - (7x^2 + 5x) = -13x^2 + 2x$

3) $(9x + 6) - (4x + 4) = 5x + 2$

4) $(2x^2 + 7x) - (2x^2 + 3x) = 0x^2 + 4x$

5) $(7x^2 + 6x) + (3x^2 - 4x) = 10x^2 + 2x$

6) $(-8x + 6) + (4x - 4) = -4x + 2$

7) $(6x^2 + 3x) + (4x^2 - 2x) = 10x^2 + 1x$

8) $(9x^2 + 6x) - (7x^2 + 4x) = 2x^2 + 2x$

9) $(5x^2 + 8x) + (3x^2 - 6x) = 8x^2 + 2x$

10) $(-2x^2 + 7x) - (2x^2 + 5x) = -4x^2 + 2x$

11) $(-4x + 6) + (2x - 4) = -2x + 2$

12) $(-3x + 5) + (2x - 3) = -1x + 2$

13) $(5x^2 + 9x) - (3x^2 + 7x) = 2x^2 + 2x$

Multiplying Monomials

✏️ **Simplify each expression.**

1) $-9x^2y^3z \times 5x =$

2) $9xy \times 4x^2y =$

3) $-4xy \times (-2z) =$

4) $8x^2y^3z \times 5x =$

5) $5x^2y^3z \times 4x =$

6) $2x^2y^2z \times 2xz^2 =$

7) $-5xy \times (-3z) =$

8) $-8x^2y^2z \times 7xz^2 =$

9) $9x^2y^2z \times 5xz^2 =$

10) $5xy \times 2x^2y =$

11) $-6x^2y^2z \times 7xz^2 =$

12) $2xy \times 4x^2y =$

13) $-3x^2y^2z \times 4xz^2 =$

14) $7xy \times 2x^2y =$

15) $-1xy \times 3x^2y =$

16) $-10x^2y^2z \times 4xz^2 =$

17) $-8xy \times (-3z) =$

18) $2x^2y^3z \times 3x =$

19) $-5xy \times 4x^2y =$

20) $-5x^2y^2z \times 5xz^2 =$

21) $8x^2y^2z \times 7xz^2 =$

22) $3x^2y^3z \times 3x =$

Answers of Multiplying Monomials

✏️ **Simplify each expression.**

1) $-9x^2y^3z \times 5x = -45x^3y^3z$

2) $9xy \times 4x^2y = 36x^3y^2$

3) $-4xy \times (-2z) = 8xyz$

4) $8x^2y^3z \times 5x = 40x^3y^3z$

5) $5x^2y^3z \times 4x = 20x^3y^3z$

6) $2x^2y^2z \times 2xz^2 = 4x^3y^2z^3$

7) $-5xy \times (-3z) = 15xyz$

8) $-8x^2y^2z \times 7xz^2 = -56x^3y^2z^3$

9) $9x^2y^2z \times 5xz^2 = 45x^3y^2z^3$

10) $5xy \times 2x^2y = 10x^3y^2$

11) $-6x^2y^2z \times 7xz^2 = -42x^3y^2z^3$

12) $2xy \times 4x^2y = 8x^3y^2$

13) $-3x^2y^2z \times 4xz^2 = -12x^3y^2z^3$

14) $7xy \times 2x^2y = 14x^3y^2$

15) $-1xy \times 3x^2y = -3x^3y^2$

16) $-10x^2y^2z \times 4xz^2 = -40x^3y^2z^3$

17) $-8xy \times (-3z) = 24xyz$

18) $2x^2y^3z \times 3x = 6x^3y^3z$

19) $-5xy \times 4x^2y = -20x^3y^2$

20) $-5x^2y^2z \times 5xz^2 = -25x^3y^2z^3$

21) $8x^2y^2z \times 7xz^2 = 56x^3y^2z^3$

22) $3x^2y^3z \times 3x = 9x^3y^3z$

Multiplying Binomials

✏️ **Find the equation of the line passing through the given points.**

1) $(-9x - 4)(-1x + 4) =$

2) $(-8x - 3)(-3x + 2) =$

3) $(-10x - 10)(3x + 5) =$

4) $(-6x - 1)(3x + 1) =$

5) $(-3x - 10)(-4x + 1) =$

6) $(-9x - 7)(1x + 1) =$

7) $(-8x - 8)(-5x + 5) =$

8) $(-1x - 4)(1x + 5) =$

9) $(-10x - 5)(-3x + 5) =$

10) $(-9x - 2)(-4x + 5) =$

11) $(-7x - 3)(5x + 5) =$

12) $(-5x - 2)(-1x + 5) =$

13) $(-9x - 3)(-3x + 3) =$

Answers of Multiplying Binomials

✏️ **Find the equation of the line passing through the given points.**

1) $(-9x - 4)(-1x + 4) = 9x^2 - 32x - 16$

2) $(-8x - 3)(-3x + 2) = 24x^2 - 7x - 6$

3) $(-10x - 10)(3x + 5) = -30x^2 - 80x - 50$

4) $(-6x - 1)(3x + 1) = -18x^2 - 9x - 1$

5) $(-3x - 10)(-4x + 1) = 12x^2 + 37x - 10$

6) $(-9x - 7)(1x + 1) = -9x^2 - 16x - 7$

7) $(-8x - 8)(-5x + 5) = 40x^2 x - 40$

8) $(-1x - 4)(1x + 5) = -1x^2 - 9x - 20$

9) $(-10x - 5)(-3x + 5) = 30x^2 - 35x - 25$

10) $(-9x - 2)(-4x + 5) = 36x^2 - 37x - 10$

11) $(-7x - 3)(5x + 5) = -35x^2 - 50x - 15$

12) $(-5x - 2)(-1x + 5) = 5x^2 - 23x - 10$

13) $(-9x - 3)(-3x + 3) = 27x^2 - 18x - 9$

Factoring Trinomials

▶ Factor each trinomial.

1) $x^2 - 121 =$

2) $x^2 - 7x - 18 =$

3) $x^2 + 5x - 36 =$

4) $x^2 - 6x - 16 =$

5) $x^2 + 13x + 36 =$

6) $-12x^2 - 26x - 12 =$

7) $x^2 - 6x + 5 =$

8) $x^2 + 10x + 25 =$

9) $x^2 - 1x - 20 =$

10) $x^2 - 6x + 5 =$

11) $x^2 + 4x - 45 =$

12) $x^2 - 5x - 14 =$

13) $2x^2 + 3x - 5 =$

14) $x^2 + 8x + 15 =$

15) $x^2 - 64 =$

16) $x^2 - 2x - 15 =$

17) $x^2 - 2x - 15 =$

18) $-10x^2 - 24x - 8 =$

19) $x^2 - 9x + 18 =$

20) $x^2 - 4x - 5 =$

21) $x^2 - 11x + 18 =$

22) $x^2 - 9x + 14 =$

Answers of Factoring Trinomials

✏️ **Factor each trinomial.**

1) $x^2 - 121 = (x+11)(x-11)$

2) $x^2 - 7x - 18 = (x-9)(x+2)$

3) $x^2 + 5x - 36 = (x-4)(x+9)$

4) $x^2 - 6x - 16 = (x+2)(x-8)$

5) $x^2 + 13x + 36 = (x+4)(x+9)$

6) $-12x^2 - 26x - 12 = (-4x-6)(3x+2)$

7) $x^2 - 6x + 5 = (x-1)(x-5)$

8) $x^2 + 10x + 25 = (x+5)(x+5)$

9) $x^2 - 1x - 20 = (x-5)(x+4)$

10) $x^2 - 6x + 5 = (x-5)(x-1)$

11) $x^2 + 4x - 45 = (x-5)(x+9)$

12) $x^2 - 5x - 14 = (x-7)(x+2)$

13) $2x^2 + 3x - 5 = (-2x-5)(-x+1)$

14) $x^2 + 8x + 15 = (x+3)(x+5)$

15) $x^2 - 64 = (x-8)(x+8)$

16) $x^2 - 2x - 15 = (x-5)(x+3)$

17) $x^2 - 2x - 15 = (x+3)(x-5)$

18) $-10x^2 - 24x - 8 = (-10x-4)(x+2)$

19) $x^2 - 9x + 18 = (x-6)(x-3)$

20) $x^2 - 4x - 5 = (x-5)(x+1)$

21) $x^2 - 11x + 18 = (x-9)(x-2)$

22) $x^2 - 9x + 14 = (x-7)(x-2)$

Dividing Monomials

✏️ **Simplify each expression.**

1) $4x^2y^3 \div 2y =$

2) $\frac{-28x^2y^3z}{4yz} =$

3) $\frac{27xzy}{-3yz} =$

4) $-30xz^2 \div 3xz^2 =$

5) $\frac{-12x^2y^3z}{2yz} =$

6) $-24x^2y^3 \div 3y =$

7) $\frac{-14xzy}{-2yz} =$

8) $-8xz^2 \div 4xz^2 =$

9) $\frac{-9xzy}{-3yz} =$

10) $-8xz^2 \div 2xz^2 =$

11) $6xz^2 \div 3xz^2 =$

12) $\frac{-8x^2y^3z}{2yz} =$

13) $\frac{-24xzy}{-4yz} =$

14) $\frac{32x^2y^3z}{4yz} =$

15) $-32xz^2 \div 4xz^2 =$

16) $-8x^2y^3 \div 4y =$

17) $24xz^2 \div 4xz^2 =$

18) $\frac{14xzy}{-2yz} =$

19) $-9xz^2 \div 3xz^2 =$

20) $12xz^2 \div 3xz^2 =$

21) $27xz^2 \div 3xz^2 =$

22) $\frac{-16x^2y^3z}{2yz} =$

Answers of Dividing Monomials

✏️ **Simplify each expression.**

1) $4x^2y^3 \div 2y = 2x^2y^2$

2) $\frac{-28x^2y^3z}{4yz} = -7x^2y^2$

3) $\frac{27xzy}{-3yz} = -9x$

4) $-30xz^2 \div 3xz^2 = -10$

5) $\frac{-12x^2y^3z}{2yz} = -6x^2y^2$

6) $-24x^2y^3 \div 3y = -8x^2y^2$

7) $\frac{-14xzy}{-2yz} = 7x$

8) $-8xz^2 \div 4xz^2 = -2$

9) $\frac{-9xzy}{-3yz} = 3x$

10) $-8xz^2 \div 2xz^2 = -4$

11) $6xz^2 \div 3xz^2 = 2$

12) $\frac{-8x^2y^3z}{2yz} = -4x^2y^2$

13) $\frac{-24xzy}{-4yz} = 6x$

14) $\frac{32x^2y^3z}{4yz} = 8x^2y^2$

15) $-32xz^2 \div 4xz^2 = -8$

16) $-8x^2y^3 \div 4y = -2x^2y^2$

17) $24xz^2 \div 4xz^2 = 6$

18) $\frac{14xzy}{-2yz} = -7x$

19) $-9xz^2 \div 3xz^2 = -3$

20) $12xz^2 \div 3xz^2 = 4$

21) $27xz^2 \div 3xz^2 = 9$

22) $\frac{-16x^2y^3z}{2yz} = -8x^2y^2$

Scientific Notation

✎ **Write each number in scientific notation.**

1) $0.748 =$

2) $0.029 =$

3) $0.581 =$

4) $848,000,000 =$

5) $887,000,000 =$

6) $0.000366 =$

7) $43,900,000 =$

8) $0.0236 =$

9) $651,000,000 =$

10) $0.0869 =$

11) $436,000,000 =$

12) $569,000 =$

13) $845,000,000 =$

14) $381,000 =$

15) $77,800,000 =$

16) $0.0733 =$

17) $0.878 =$

18) $0.000363 =$

19) $46,000,000 =$

20) $0.00345 =$

21) $757,000 =$

22) $484,000 =$

Answers of Scientific Notation

✏️ **Write each number in scientific notation.**

1) $0.748 = 7.48 \times 10^{-1}$

2) $0.029 = 2.9 \times 10^{-2}$

3) $0.581 = 5.81 \times 10^{-1}$

4) $848,000,000 = 8.48 \times 10^{8}$

5) $887,000,000 = 8.87 \times 10^{8}$

6) $0.000366 = 3.66 \times 10^{-4}$

7) $43,900,000 = 4.39 \times 10^{7}$

8) $0.0236 = 2.36 \times 10^{-2}$

9) $651,000,000 = 6.51 \times 10^{8}$

10) $0.0869 = 8.69 \times 10^{-2}$

11) $436,000,000 = 4.36 \times 10^{8}$

12) $569,000 = 5.69 \times 10^{5}$

13) $845,000,000 = 8.45 \times 10^{8}$

14) $381,000 = 3.81 \times 10^{5}$

15) $77,800,000 = 7.78 \times 10^{7}$

16) $0.0733 = 7.33 \times 10^{-2}$

17) $0.878 = 8.78 \times 10^{-1}$

18) $0.000363 = 3.63 \times 10^{-4}$

19) $46,000,000 = 4.6 \times 10^{7}$

20) $0.00345 = 3.45 \times 10^{-3}$

21) $757,000 = 7.57 \times 10^{5}$

22) $484,000 = 4.84 \times 10^{5}$

Mean, Median, Mode, and Range of the Given Data

✏️ **Find Mean, Median, Mode, and Range of the Given Data.**

1) 10, 24, 17, 3, 6, 56, 6

2) 2, 54, 13, 24, 17, 6, 6

3) 15, 7, 10, 7, 2, 31, 20

4) 10, 20, 16, 4, 5, 26, 5

5) 3, 57, 10, 21, 17, 5, 5

6) 13, 21, 19, 3, 8, 62, 8

7) 16, 7, 10, 7, 3, 49, 20

8) 12, 21, 18, 1, 8, 32, 8

9) 1, 63, 11, 21, 16, 5, 5

10) 16, 6, 13, 6, 1, 43, 20

11) 12, 22, 19, 3, 5, 29, 5

12) 14, 21, 17, 2, 9, 38, 9

13) 16, 5, 10, 5, 1, 37, 20

Answers of Mean, Median, Mode, and Range of the Given Data

✏️ **Find Mean, Median, Mode, and Range of the Given Data.**

1) 10, 24, 17, 3, 6, 56, 6 ⇒ mean: 17.43, median: 10, mode: 6, range : 21

2) 2, 54, 13, 24, 17, 6, 6 ⇒ mean: 17.43, median: 13, mode: 6, range : 22

3) 15, 7, 10, 7, 2, 31, 20 ⇒ mean: 13.14, median: 10, mode: 7, range : 18

4) 10, 20, 16, 4, 5, 26, 5 ⇒ mean: 12.29, median: 10, mode: 5, range : 16

5) 3, 57, 10, 21, 17, 5, 5 ⇒ mean: 16.86, median: 10, mode: 5, range : 18

6) 13, 21, 19, 3, 8, 62, 8 ⇒ mean: 19.14, median: 13, mode: 8, range : 18

7) 16, 7, 10, 7, 3, 49, 20 ⇒ mean: 16, median: 10, mode: 7, range : 17

8) 12, 21, 18, 1, 8, 32, 8 ⇒ mean: 14.29, median: 12, mode: 8, range : 20

9) 1, 63, 11, 21, 16, 5, 5 ⇒ mean: 17.43, median: 11, mode: 5, range : 20

10) 16, 6, 13, 6, 1, 43, 20 ⇒ mean: 15, median: 13, mode: 6, range : 19

11) 12, 22, 19, 3, 5, 29, 5 ⇒ mean: 13.57, median: 12, mode: 5, range : 19

12) 14, 21, 17, 2, 9, 38, 9 ⇒ mean: 15.71, median: 14, mode: 9, range : 19

13) 16, 5, 10, 5, 1, 37, 20 ⇒ mean: 13.43, median: 10, mode: 5, range : 19

The Pie Graph or Circle Graph

 Pie Graph

1) What percentage of pie graph is yellow?

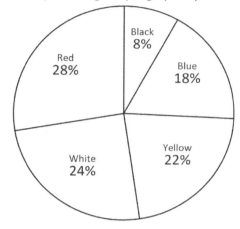

2) Which color is the most?

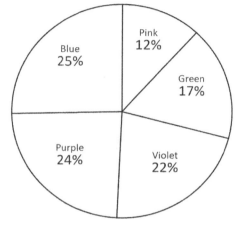

3) Which color is the least?

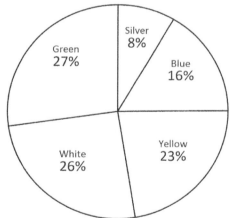

4) What percent of people voted for Sepehr?

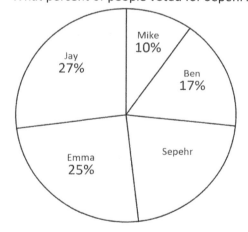

5) Which color is the most?

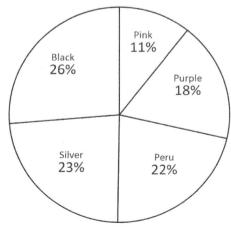

6) What percentage of pie graph is black?

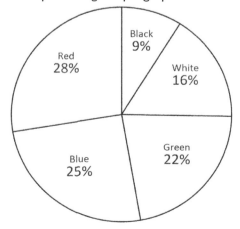

Answers of The Pie Graph or Circle Graph

Pie Graph

1) What percentage of pie graph is yellow? 22%

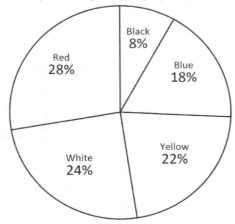

2) Which color is the most? Blue

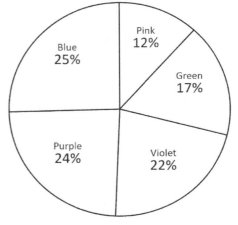

3) Which color is the least? Silver

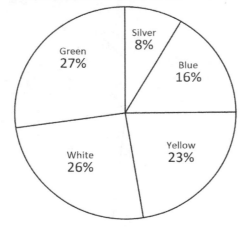

4) What percent of people voted for Sepehr? 21%

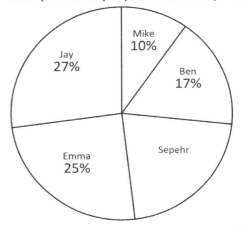

5) Which color is the most? Black

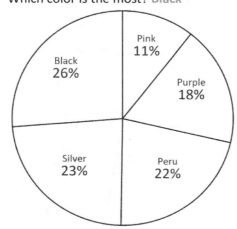

6) What percentage of pie graph is black? 9%

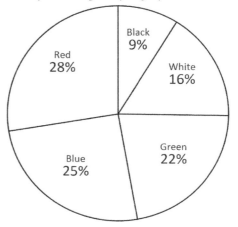

Probability Problems

Solve.

1) A number is chosen at random from 1 to 13. Find the probability of selecting a 6 or smaller.

2) A number is chosen at random from 1 to 26. Find the probability of selecting a 6 or smaller.

3) A number is chosen at random from 1 to 15. Find the probability of selecting a 2 or smaller.

4) Bag A contains 22 red marbles and 6 green marbles. Bag B contains 5 black marbles and 9 orange marbles. What is the probability of selecting a green marble at random from bag A? What is the probability of selecting a black marble at random from Bag B?

5) A number is chosen at random from 1 to 44. Find the probability of selecting prime numbers.

6) Bag A contains 8 red marbles and 9 green marbles. Bag B contains 9 black marbles and 1 orange marbles. What is the probability of selecting a green marble at random from bag A? What is the probability of selecting a black marble at random from Bag B?

7) A number is chosen at random from 1 to 38. Find the probability of selecting prime numbers.

8) A number is chosen at random from 1 to 20. Find the probability of selecting prime numbers.

9) A number is chosen at random from 1 to 34. Find the probability of selecting prime numbers.

10) A number is chosen at random from 1 to 30. Find the probability of selecting prime numbers.

Answers of Probability Problems

✏️ **Solve.**

1) A number is chosen at random from 1 to 13. Find the probability of selecting a 6 or smaller.
$\frac{6}{13}$

2) A number is chosen at random from 1 to 26. Find the probability of selecting a 6 or smaller.
$\frac{3}{13}$

3) A number is chosen at random from 1 to 15. Find the probability of selecting a 2 or smaller.
$\frac{2}{15}$

4) Bag A contains 22 red marbles and 6 green marbles. Bag B contains 5 black marbles and 9 orange marbles. What is the probability of selecting a green marble at random from bag A? What is the probability of selecting a black marble at random from Bag B? $\frac{3}{14}, \frac{5}{14}$

5) A number is chosen at random from 1 to 44. Find the probability of selecting prime numbers. $\frac{7}{22}$

6) Bag A contains 8 red marbles and 9 green marbles. Bag B contains 9 black marbles and 1 orange marbles. What is the probability of selecting a green marble at random from bag A? What is the probability of selecting a black marble at random from Bag B? $\frac{9}{17}, \frac{9}{10}$

7) A number is chosen at random from 1 to 38. Find the probability of selecting prime numbers. $\frac{6}{19}$

8) A number is chosen at random from 1 to 20. Find the probability of selecting prime numbers. $\frac{2}{5}$

9) A number is chosen at random from 1 to 34. Find the probability of selecting prime numbers. $\frac{11}{34}$

10) A number is chosen at random from 1 to 30. Find the probability of selecting prime numbers. $\frac{1}{3}$

The Pythagorean Theorem

✏️ **Find each missing length.**

1) $x = $

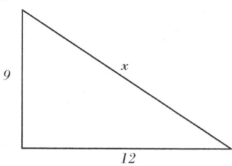

2) $x = $

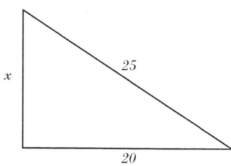

3) $x = $

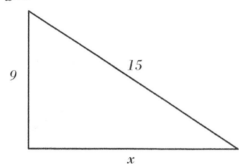

4) $x = $

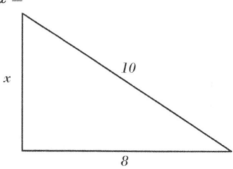

5) $x = $

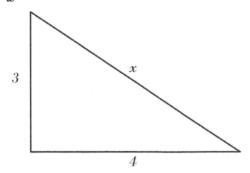

6) $x = $

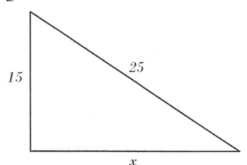

Answers of The Pythagorean Theorem

✏️ **Find each missing length.**

1) $x = 15$

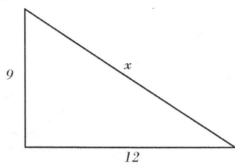

2) $x = 15$

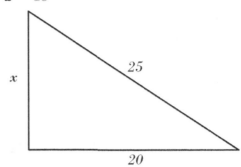

3) $x = 12$

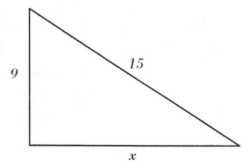

4) $x = 6$

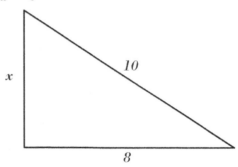

5) $x = 5$

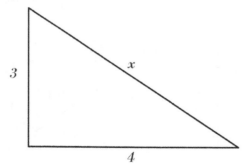

6) $x = 20$

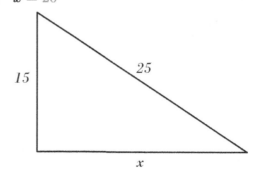

Angle and Area of Triangles

✏️ **Find the area of each.**

1) What is the area of the triangle?

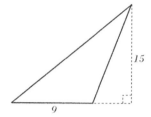

2) What is the area of the triangle?

3) What is the area of the triangle?

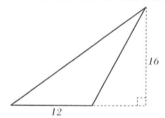

4) What is the area of the triangle?

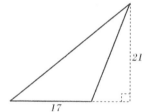

✏️ **Find the measure of the unknown angle in each triangle.**

1) What is the unknown angle (α)?

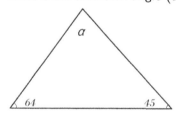

2) What is the unknown angle (α)?

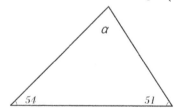

3) What is the unknown angle (α)?

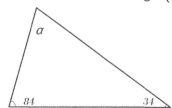

4) What is the unknown angle (α)?

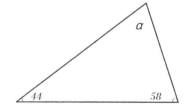

Answers of Angle and Area of Triangles

✏️ **Find the area of each.**

1) $x = 67.5 \text{ m}^2$

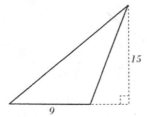

2) $x = 262.5 \text{ m}^2$

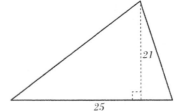

3) $x = 96 \text{ m}^2$

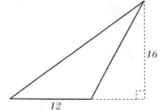

4) $x = 178.5 \text{ m}^2$

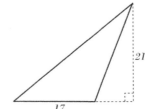

✏️ **Find the measure of the unknown angle in each triangle.**

1) $\alpha = 71$

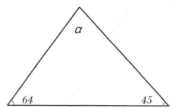

2) $\alpha = 75$

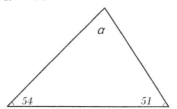

3) $\alpha = 62$

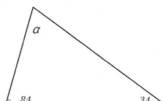

4) $\alpha = 78$

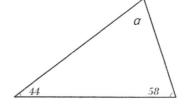

Perimeter of Polygons

Find the perimeter of each shape.

1) What is the perimeter of the following regular hexagon?

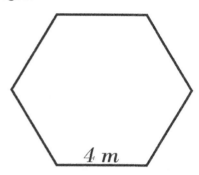

2) What is the perimeter of the following equilateral triangle?

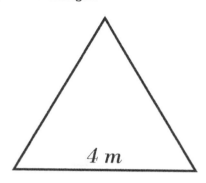

3) What is the perimeter of the following regular hexagon?

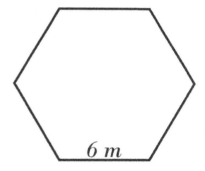

4) What is the perimeter of the following rectangle?

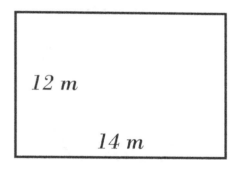

5) What is the perimeter of the following regular hexagon?

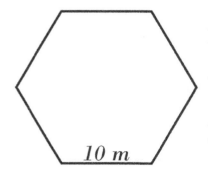

6) What is the perimeter of the following rectangle?

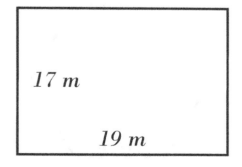

Answers of Perimeter of Polygons

✏️ **Find the perimeter of each shape.**

1) What is the perimeter of the following regular hexagon? $24\ m$

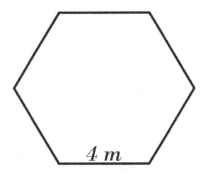
4 m

2) What is the perimeter of the following equilateral triangle? $12\ m$

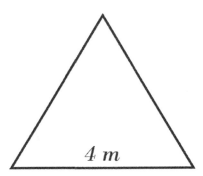
4 m

3) What is the perimeter of the following regular hexagon? $36\ m$

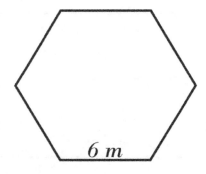
6 m

4) What is the perimeter of the following rectangle? $52\ m$

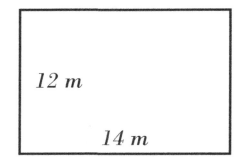
12 m
14 m

5) What is the perimeter of the following regular hexagon? $60\ m$

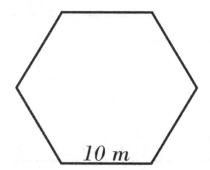
10 m

6) What is the perimeter of the following rectangle? $72\ m$

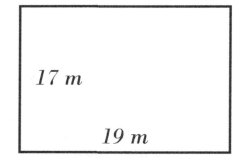
17 m
19 m

Area and Circumference of Circles

✏️ **Find the area and circumference of each.**

1)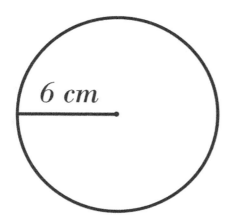

2)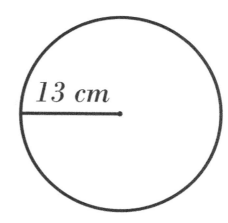

3)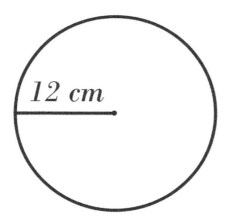

4)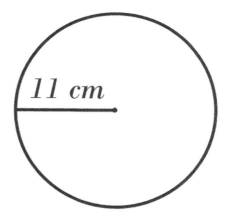

5)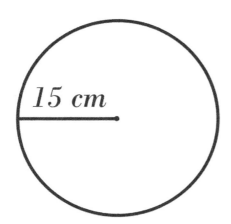

6)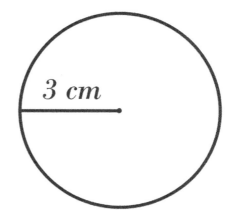

Answers of Area and Circumference of Circles

✏️ **Find the area and circumference of each.**

1) Area: 113.04 cm², Circumference: 37.68 cm   2) Area: 530.66 cm², Circumference: 81.64 cm

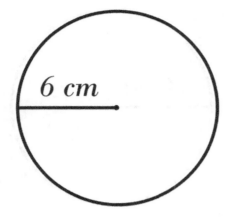 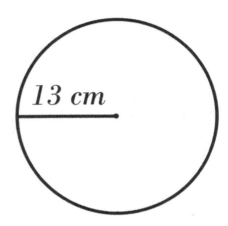

3) Area: 452.16 cm², Circumference: 75.36 cm   4) Area: 379.94 cm², Circumference: 69.08 cm

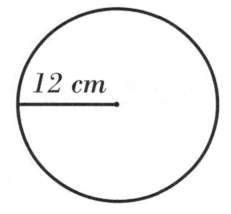 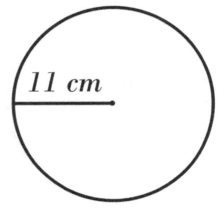

5) Area: 706.5 cm², Circumference: 94.2 cm   6) Area: 28.26 cm², Circumference: 18.84 cm

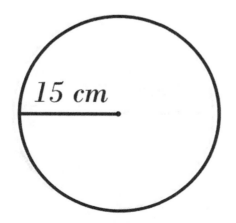 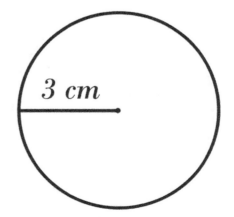

Area of Squares, Rectangles, and Parallelograms

✏️ **Find the area of each.**

1)
13 cm
16 cm

2)
20 cm
23 cm

3)
17 cm
21 cm

4)
11 cm

5)
6 cm

6)
19 cm
23 cm

Answers of Area of Squares, Rectangles, and Parallelograms

✏️ **Find the area of each.**

1) 208 cm^2

   13 cm
   16 cm

2) 460 cm^2

   20 cm
   23 cm

3) 357 cm^2

   17 cm
   21 cm

4) 121 cm^2

   11 cm

5) 36 cm^2

   6 cm

6) 437 cm^2

   19 cm
   23 cm

Area of Trapezoids

✏️ **Find the area of each trapezoid.**

1)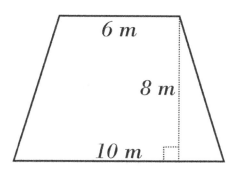

2)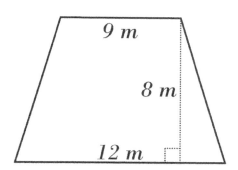

3)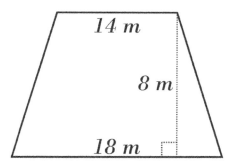

4)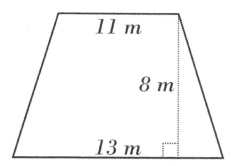

5)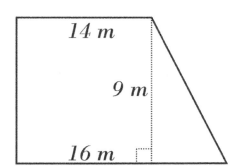

6)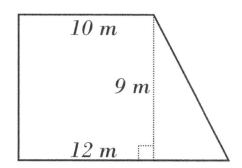

Answers of Area of Trapezoids

✏️ **Find the area of each trapezoid.**

1) $64\ m^2$

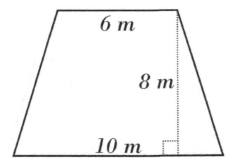

2) $84\ m^2$

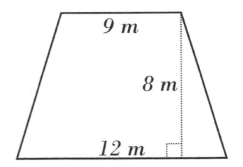

3) $128\ m^2$

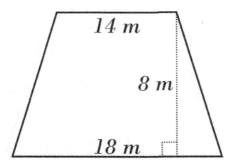

4) $96\ m^2$

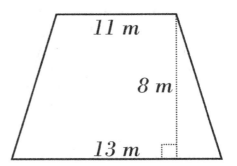

5) $135\ m^2$

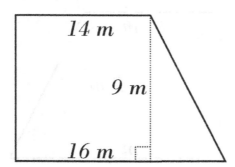

6) $99\ m^2$

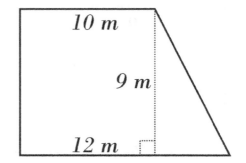

Angles

✏️ **Find the value of x in the following figures.**

1)
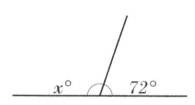

2)
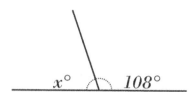

3)
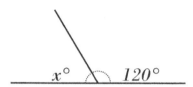

4)
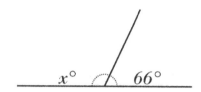

5)
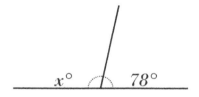

6)
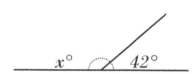

7)
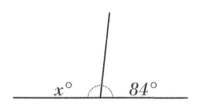

8)
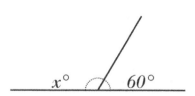

9)
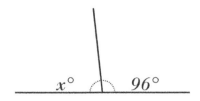

10)
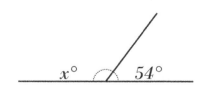

Answers of Angles

✏️ **Find the value of x in the following figures.**

1) 108°

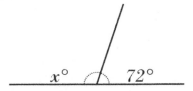

2) 72°

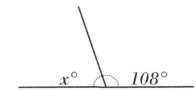

3) 60°

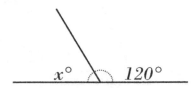

4) 114°

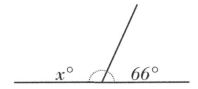

5) 102°

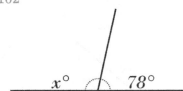

6) 138°

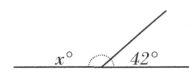

7) 96°

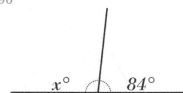

8) 120°

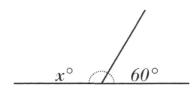

9) 84°

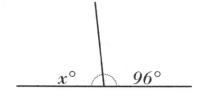

10) 126°

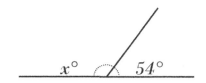

Volume of Cubes

✏️ **Find the volume of each.**

1)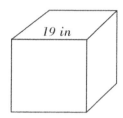

2)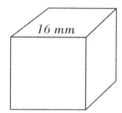

3)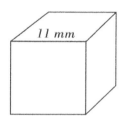

4)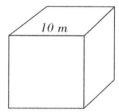

5)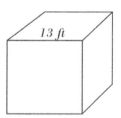

6)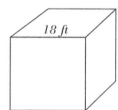

7)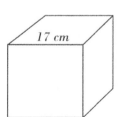

8)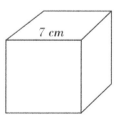

9)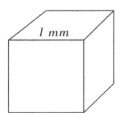

10)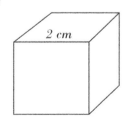

Answers of Volume of Cubes

✏️ **Find the volume of each.**

1) 6859 in³

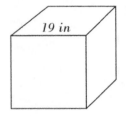

2) 4096 mm³

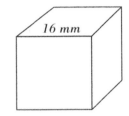

3) 1331 mm³

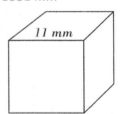

4) 1000 m³

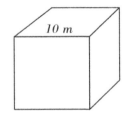

5) 2197 ft³

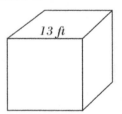

6) 5832 ft³

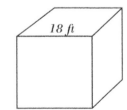

7) 4913 cm³

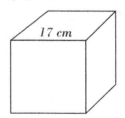

8) 343 cm³

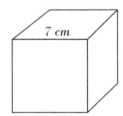

9) 1 mm³

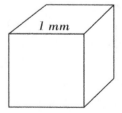

10) 8 cm³

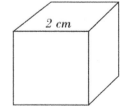

Volume of Rectangle Prisms

✏️ **Find the volume of each rectangular prisms.**

1)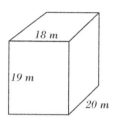

2)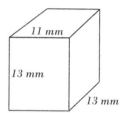

3)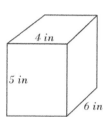

4)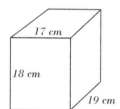

5)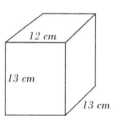

6)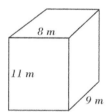

7)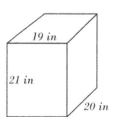

8)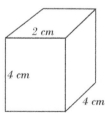

9)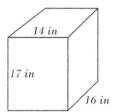

10)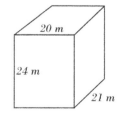

Answers of Volume of Rectangle Prisms

✏️ **Find the volume of each rectangular prisms.**

1) 6840 m³
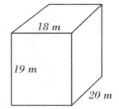

2) 1859 mm³
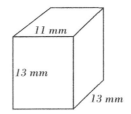

3) 120 in³
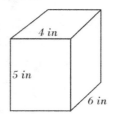

4) 5814 cm³
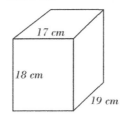

5) 2028 cm³
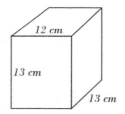

6) 792 m³
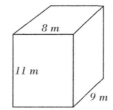

7) 7980 in³
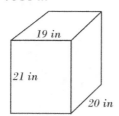

8) 32 cm³
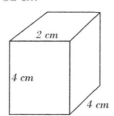

9) 3808 in³
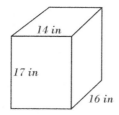

10) 10080 m³
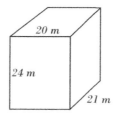

Volume and Surface Area of Cubes

✏️ **Find the surface area of each cube.**

1)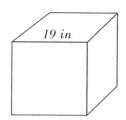

2)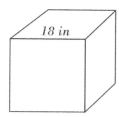

3)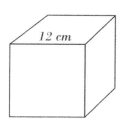

4)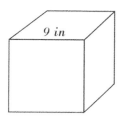

5)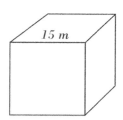

6)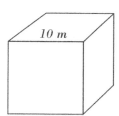

7)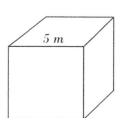

8)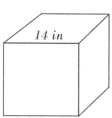

9)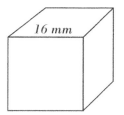

10)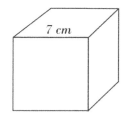

Answers of volume and Surface Area of Cubes

✏️ **Find the surface area of each cube.**

1) 2166 in²

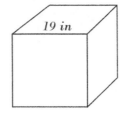

2) 1944 in²

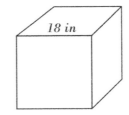

3) 864 cm²

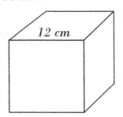

4) 486 in²

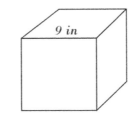

5) 1350 m²

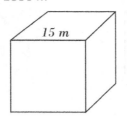

6) 600 m²

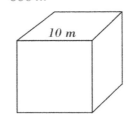

7) 150 m²

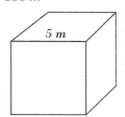

8) 1176 in²

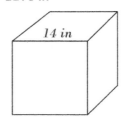

9) 1536 mm²

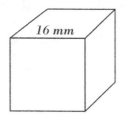

10) 294 cm²

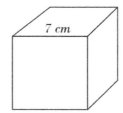

Surface Area of a Rectangle Prism

✏️ **Find the surface area of each prism.**

1)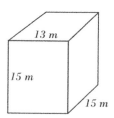

2)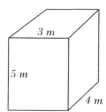

3)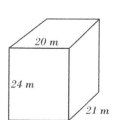

4)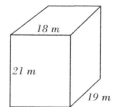

5)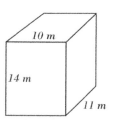

6)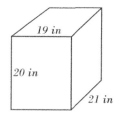

7)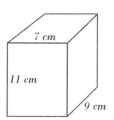

8)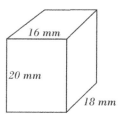

9)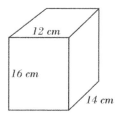

10)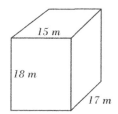

Answers of Surface Area of a Rectangle Prism

 Find the surface area of each prism.

1) 1230 m²

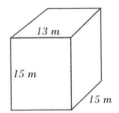

2) 94 m²

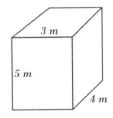

3) 2808 m²

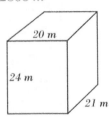

4) 2238 m²

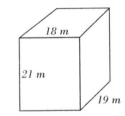

5) 808 m²

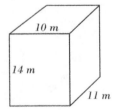

6) 2398 in²

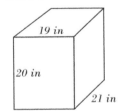

7) 478 cm²

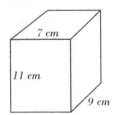

8) 1936 mm²

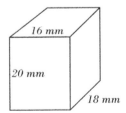

9) 1168 cm²

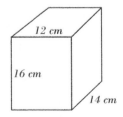

10) 1662 m²

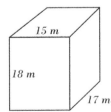

Volume of a Cylinder

Find the volume of each cylinder.

1)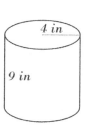

2)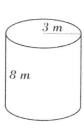

3)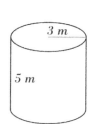

4)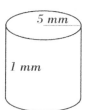

5)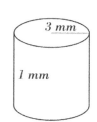

6)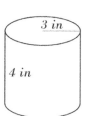

7)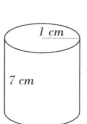

8)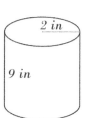

9)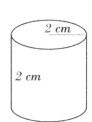

10)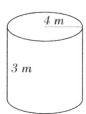

Answers of Volume of a Cylinder

✏️ **Find the volume of each cylinder.**

1) 452.16 in³

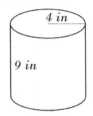

2) 226.08 m³

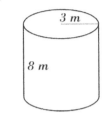

3) 141.3 m³

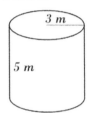

4) 78.5 mm³

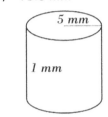

5) 28.26 mm³

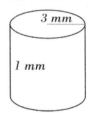

6) 113.04 in³

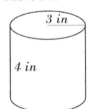

7) 21.98 cm³

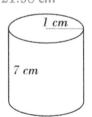

8) 113.04 in³

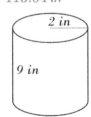

9) 25.12 cm³

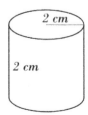

10) 150.72 m³

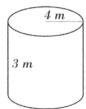

Surface Area of a Cylinder

✏️ **Find the surface are of each cylinder.**

1) 1 mm (top), 1 mm (height)

2) 2 cm (top), 7 cm (height)

3) 3 m (top), 3 m (height)

4) 3 in (top), 9 in (height)

5) 4 m (top), 3 m (height)

6) 6 m (top), 10 m (height)

7) 5 m (top), 5 m (height)

8) 2 m (top), 5 m (height)

9) 4 mm (top), 6 mm (height)

10) 4 mm (top), 1 mm (height)

Answers of Surface Area of a Cylinder

 Find the surface are of each cylinder.

1) 12.56 mm²
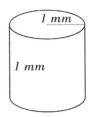

2) 113.04 cm²
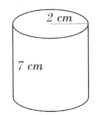

3) 113.04 m²
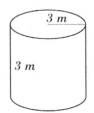

4) 226.08 in²
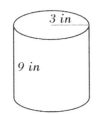

5) 175.84 m²
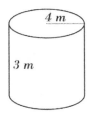

6) 602.88 m²
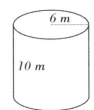

7) 314 m²
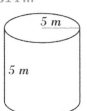

8) 87.92 m²
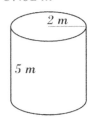

9) 251.2 mm²
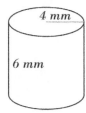

10) 125.6 mm²
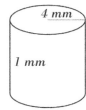

Function Notation

▶ **Evaluate each function.**

1) $h(x) = 3x^2 + 5$, find $h(5)$

2) $h(x) = 3x^2 - x + 3$, find $h(9)$

3) $m(u) = 5u^2 + u + 7$, find $m(6)$

4) $h(x) = 8x^2 + 2$, find $h(1)$

5) $f(x) = 11x^2 - x + 2$, find $f(4)$

6) $f(x) = 11x^2 + 4$, find $f(1)$

7) $g(t) = 2t^2 - t + 2$, find $g(2)$

8) $h(x) = 8x^2 + x + 3$, find $h(8)$

9) $m(u) = 10u^2 + 2$, find $m(6)$

10) $h(x) = 3x^2 + x + 4$, find $h(1)$

11) $g(t) = 7t^2 + 1$, find $g(1)$

12) $m(u) = 10u^2 - u + 8$, find $m(6)$

13) $p(s) = 4s + 2$, find $p(8)$

14) $f(x) = 6x^2 - x + 8$, find $f(7)$

15) $p(s) = 9s + 8$, find $p(3)$

16) $g(t) = 7t^2 - t + 6$, find $g(2)$

17) $g(t) = 7t^2 + t + 7$, find $g(6)$

18) $f(x) = 6x + 7$, find $f(8)$

19) $g(t) = 2t^2 + t + 4$, find $g(2)$

20) $p(s) = 4s^2 - s + 9$, find $p(9)$

21) $m(u) = 5u + 3$, find $m(2)$

22) $p(s) = 9s^2 + s + 2$, find $p(3)$

Answers of Function Notation

✏️ **Evaluate each function.**

1) $h(x) = 3x^2 + 5$, find $h(5)$
   ⇒ $h(5) = 80$

2) $h(x) = 3x^2 - x + 3$, find $h(9)$
   ⇒ $h(9) = 237$

3) $m(u) = 5u^2 + u + 7$, find $m(6)$
   ⇒ $m(6) = 193$

4) $h(x) = 8x^2 + 2$, find $h(1)$
   ⇒ $h(1) = 10$

5) $f(x) = 11x^2 - x + 2$, find $f(4)$
   ⇒ $f(4) = 174$

6) $f(x) = 11x^2 + 4$, find $f(1)$
   ⇒ $f(1) = 15$

7) $g(t) = 2t^2 - t + 2$, find $g(2)$
   ⇒ $g(2) = 8$

8) $h(x) = 8x^2 + x + 3$, find $h(8)$
   ⇒ $h(8) = 523$

9) $m(u) = 10u^2 + 2$, find $m(6)$
   ⇒ $m(6) = 362$

10) $h(x) = 3x^2 + x + 4$, find $h(1)$
    ⇒ $h(1) = 8$

11) $g(t) = 7t^2 + 1$, find $g(1)$
    ⇒ $g(1) = 8$

12) $m(u) = 10u^2 - u + 8$, find $m(6)$
    ⇒ $m(6) = 362$

13) $p(s) = 4s + 2$, find $p(8)$
    ⇒ $p(8) = 34$

14) $f(x) = 6x^2 - x + 8$, find $f(7)$
    ⇒ $f(7) = 295$

15) $p(s) = 9s + 8$, find $p(3)$
    ⇒ $p(3) = 35$

16) $g(t) = 7t^2 - t + 6$, find $g(2)$
    ⇒ $g(2) = 32$

17) $g(t) = 7t^2 + t + 7$, find $g(6)$
    ⇒ $g(6) = 265$

18) $f(x) = 6x + 7$, find $f(8)$
    ⇒ $f(8) = 55$

19) $g(t) = 2t^2 + t + 4$, find $g(2)$
    ⇒ $g(2) = 14$

20) $p(s) = 4s^2 - s + 9$, find $p(9)$
    ⇒ $p(9) = 324$

21) $m(u) = 5u + 3$, find $m(2)$
    ⇒ $m(2) = 13$

22) $p(s) = 9s^2 + s + 2$, find $p(3)$
    ⇒ $p(3) = 86$

Adding and Subtracting Functions

✏️ **Perform the indicated operation.**

1) $h(x) = -4x + 6$
   $g(x) = 8x + 1$
   Find $(h - g)(x)$

2) $h(x) = -3x + 5$
   $g(x) = 2x + 4$
   Find $(h + g)(x)$

3) $h(x) = -2x + 6$
   $g(x) = 3x + 4$
   Find $(h - g)(x)$

4) $h(x) = 4x + 8$
   $g(x) = 2x + 3$
   Find $(h + g)(x)$

5) $h(x) = -2x + 8$
   $g(x) = 7x + 4$
   Find $(h - g)(x)$

6) $h(x) = -10x + 6$
   $g(x) = 3x + 4$
   Find $(h - g)(x)$

7) $h(x) = -8x + 6$
   $g(x) = 2x + 2$
   Find $(h - g)(x)$

8) $h(x) = -2x + 5$
   $g(x) = 7x + 1$
   Find $(h + g)(x)$

9) $h(x) = 11x + 7$
   $g(x) = 7x + 4$
   Find $(h + g)(x)$

10) $h(x) = 10x + 5$
    $g(x) = 4x + 4$
    Find $(h + g)(x)$

11) $h(x) = -3x + 7$
    $g(x) = 4x + 1$
    Find $(h - g)(x)$

12) $h(x) = -6x + 5$
    $g(x) = 2x + 4$
    Find $(h + g)(x)$

Answers of Adding and Subtracting Functions

✏️ **Perform the indicated operation.**

1) $h(x) = -4x + 6$
   $g(x) = 8x + 1$
   Find $(h - g)(x)$
   $(h - g)(x) = -12x + 5$

2) $h(x) = -3x + 5$
   $g(x) = 2x + 4$
   Find $(h + g)(x)$
   $(h + g)(x) = -1x + 9$

3) $h(x) = -2x + 6$
   $g(x) = 3x + 4$
   Find $(h - g)(x)$
   $(h - g)(x) = -5x + 2$

4) $h(x) = 4x + 8$
   $g(x) = 2x + 3$
   Find $(h + g)(x)$
   $(h + g)(x) = 6x + 11$

5) $h(x) = -2x + 8$
   $g(x) = 7x + 4$
   Find $(h - g)(x)$
   $(h - g)(x) = -9x + 4$

6) $h(x) = -10x + 6$
   $g(x) = 3x + 4$
   Find $(h - g)(x)$
   $(h - g)(x) = -13x + 2$

7) $h(x) = -8x + 6$
   $g(x) = 2x + 2$
   Find $(h - g)(x)$
   $(h - g)(x) = -10x + 4$

8) $h(x) = -2x + 5$
   $g(x) = 7x + 1$
   Find $(h + g)(x)$
   $(h + g)(x) = 5x + 6$

9) $h(x) = 11x + 7$
   $g(x) = 7x + 4$
   Find $(h + g)(x)$
   $(h + g)(x) = 18x + 11$

10) $h(x) = 10x + 5$
    $g(x) = 4x + 4$
    Find $(h + g)(x)$
    $(h + g)(x) = 14x + 9$

11) $h(x) = -3x + 7$
    $g(x) = 4x + 1$
    Find $(h - g)(x)$
    $(h - g)(x) = -7x + 6$

12) $h(x) = -6x + 5$
    $g(x) = 2x + 4$
    Find $(h + g)(x)$
    $(h + g)(x) = -4x + 9$

Multiplying and Dividing Functions

▶ **Perform the indicated operation.**

1) $h(x) = 5x$
   $g(x) = -10x^3 + 10x^2$
   Find $\left(\frac{g}{h}\right)(x)$

2) $h(x) = 10x$
   $g(x) = 6x + 4$
   Find $(h \cdot g)(3)$

3) $h(x) = 11x$
   $g(x) = 7x + 4$
   Find $(h \cdot g)(x)$

4) $h(x) = 6x$
   $g(x) = -12x^3 + 18x^2$
   Find $\left(\frac{g}{h}\right)(x)$

5) $h(x) = 7x$
   $g(x) = -21x^3 + 14x^2$
   Find $\left(\frac{g}{h}\right)(2)$

6) $h(x) = -7x$
   $g(x) = 8x - 2$
   Find $(h \cdot g)(x)$

7) $h(x) = 2x$
   $g(x) = 4x + 4$
   Find $(h \cdot g)(1)$

8) $h(x) = 9x$
   $g(x) = -27x^3 + 36x^2$
   Find $\left(\frac{g}{h}\right)(x)$

9) $h(x) = 2x$
   $g(x) = 8x^3 + 6x^2$
   Find $\left(\frac{g}{h}\right)(x)$

10) $h(x) = 3x$
    $g(x) = 6x + 4$
    Find $(h \cdot g)(3)$

11) $h(x) = -5x$
    $g(x) = 6x - 2$
    Find $(h \cdot g)(x)$

12) $h(x) = 2x$
    $g(x) = 6x + 3$
    Find $(h \cdot g)(x)$

Answers of Multiplying and Dividing Functions

✏️ **Perform the indicated operation.**

1) $h(x) = 5x$
   $g(x) = -10x^3 + 10x^2$
   Find $\left(\frac{g}{h}\right)(x)$
   $\left(\frac{g}{h}\right)(x) = -2x^2 + 2x$

2) $h(x) = 10x$
   $g(x) = 6x + 4$
   Find $(h \cdot g)(3)$
   $(h \cdot g)(x) = 660$

3) $h(x) = 11x$
   $g(x) = 7x + 4$
   Find $(h \cdot g)(x)$
   $(h \cdot g)(x) = 77x^2 + 44x$

4) $h(x) = 6x$
   $g(x) = -12x^3 + 18x^2$
   Find $\left(\frac{g}{h}\right)(x)$
   $\left(\frac{g}{h}\right)(x) = -2x^2 + 3x$

5) $h(x) = 7x$
   $g(x) = -21x^3 + 14x^2$
   Find $\left(\frac{g}{h}\right)(2)$
   $\left(\frac{g}{h}\right)(x) = -8$

6) $h(x) = -7x$
   $g(x) = 8x - 2$
   Find $(h \cdot g)(x)$
   $(h \cdot g)(x) = -56x^2 + 14x$

7) $h(x) = 2x$
   $g(x) = 4x + 4$
   Find $(h \cdot g)(1)$
   $(h \cdot g)(x) = 16$

8) $h(x) = 9x$
   $g(x) = -27x^3 + 36x^2$
   Find $\left(\frac{g}{h}\right)(x)$
   $\left(\frac{g}{h}\right)(x) = -3x^2 + 4x$

9) $h(x) = 2x$
   $g(x) = 8x^3 + 6x^2$
   Find $\left(\frac{g}{h}\right)(x)$
   $\left(\frac{g}{h}\right)(x) = 4x^2 + 3x$

10) $h(x) = 3x$
    $g(x) = 6x + 4$
    Find $(h \cdot g)(3)$
    $(h \cdot g)(x) = 198$

11) $h(x) = -5x$
    $g(x) = 6x - 2$
    Find $(h \cdot g)(x)$
    $(h \cdot g)(x) = -30x^2 + 10x$

12) $h(x) = 2x$
    $g(x) = 6x + 3$
    Find $(h \cdot g)(x)$
    $(h \cdot g)(x) = 12x^2 + 6x$

Composition of Functions

Perform the indicated operation.

1) $f(x) = 8x + 8$
   $g(x) = 4x + 3$
   Find $f(f(x)))$

2) $f(x) = 7x + 2$
   $g(x) = 2x + 3$
   Find $g(g(4)))$

3) $f(x) = 9x + 3$
   $g(x) = 5x + 1$
   Find $g(g(3)))$

4) $f(x) = 11x + 1$
   $g(x) = 6x + 1$
   Find $g(g(1)))$

5) $f(x) = 5x + 4$
   $g(x) = 7x + 2$
   Find $f(g(x)))$

6) $f(x) = 11x + 2$
   $g(x) = 2x + 1$
   Find $f(f(x)))$

7) $f(x) = 8x + 3$
   $g(x) = 2x + 2$
   Find $f(g(x)))$

8) $f(x) = 7x + 6$
   $g(x) = -2x + 3$
   Find $f(g(x)))$

9) $f(x) = 10x + 7$
   $g(x) = 6x + 4$
   Find $g(g(3)))$

10) $f(x) = 8x + 8$
    $g(x) = 3x + 2$
    Find $f(g(-3)))$

11) $f(x) = 11x + 7$
    $g(x) = 6x + 4$
    Find $f(g(-4)))$

12) $f(x) = 6x + 3$
    $g(x) = 5x + 3$
    Find $f(g(-1)))$

Answers of Composition of Functions

✏️ **Perform the indicated operation.**

1) $f(x) = 8x + 8$
   $g(x) = 4x + 3$
   Find $f(f(x)))$
   $f(g(x)) = 64x + 72$

2) $f(x) = 7x + 2$
   $g(x) = 2x + 3$
   Find $g(g(4)))$
   $g(g(4)) = 25$

3) $f(x) = 9x + 3$
   $g(x) = 5x + 1$
   Find $g(g(3)))$
   $g(g(3)) = 81$

4) $f(x) = 11x + 1$
   $g(x) = 6x + 1$
   Find $g(g(1)))$
   $g(g(1)) = 43$

5) $f(x) = 5x + 4$
   $g(x) = 7x + 2$
   Find $f(g(x)))$
   $f(g(x)) = 35x + 14$

6) $f(x) = 11x + 2$
   $g(x) = 2x + 1$
   Find $f(f(x)))$
   $f(g(x)) = 121x + 24$

7) $f(x) = 8x + 3$
   $g(x) = 2x + 2$
   Find $f(g(x)))$
   $f(g(x)) = 16x + 19$

8) $f(x) = 7x + 6$
   $g(x) = -2x + 3$
   Find $f(g(x)))$
   $f(g(x)) = -14x + 27$

9) $f(x) = 10x + 7$
   $g(x) = 6x + 4$
   Find $g(g(3)))$
   $g(g(3)) = 136$

10) $f(x) = 8x + 8$
    $g(x) = 3x + 2$
    Find $f(g(-3)))$
    $f(g(-3)) = -48$

11) $f(x) = 11x + 7$
    $g(x) = 6x + 4$
    Find $f(g(-4)))$
    $f(g(-4)) = -213$

12) $f(x) = 6x + 3$
    $g(x) = 5x + 3$
    Find $f(g(-1)))$
    $f(g(-1)) = -9$

AFOQT Math Practice Tests

AFOQT Test Review

The Air Force Officer Qualifying Test (AFOQT) is a standardized test to assess skills and personality traits that have proven to be predictive of success in officer commissioning programs such as the training program.

The AFOQT is used to select applicants for officer commissioning programs, such as Officer Training School (OTS) or Air Force Reserve Officer Training Corps (Air Force ROTC) and pilot and navigator training.

The AFOQT is a multiple-aptitude battery that measures developed abilities and helps predict future academic and occupational success in the military. The AFOQT is a multiple-choice test which consists of 12 subtests and two of them are Arithmetic Reasoning and Mathematics Knowledge.

In this section, there are 2 complete Arithmetic Reasoning and Mathematics Knowledge AFOQT Tests. Take these tests to see what score you'll be able to receive on a real AFOQT test.

AFOQT Math Practice Tests

Time to Test

Time to refine your quantitative reasoning skill with a practice test

In this section, there are two complete AFOQT Mathematics practice tests. Take these tests to simulate the test day experience. After you've finished, score your tests using the answer keys.

Before You Start

- You'll need a pencil and a timer to take the test.
- For each question, there are four possible answers. Choose which one is best.
- It's okay to guess. There is no penalty for wrong answers.
- Use the answer sheet provided to record your answers.
- After you've finished the test, review the answer key to see where you went wrong.

Calculators are NOT permitted for the AFOQT Test

Good Luck!

AFOQT Math Practice Test 1 Answer Sheet

Remove (or photocopy) this answer sheet and use it to complete the practice test

1) Ⓐ Ⓑ Ⓒ Ⓓ Ⓔ   2) Ⓐ Ⓑ Ⓒ Ⓓ Ⓔ   3) Ⓐ Ⓑ Ⓒ Ⓓ Ⓔ
4) Ⓐ Ⓑ Ⓒ Ⓓ Ⓔ   5) Ⓐ Ⓑ Ⓒ Ⓓ Ⓔ   6) Ⓐ Ⓑ Ⓒ Ⓓ Ⓔ
7) Ⓐ Ⓑ Ⓒ Ⓓ Ⓔ   8) Ⓐ Ⓑ Ⓒ Ⓓ Ⓔ   9) Ⓐ Ⓑ Ⓒ Ⓓ Ⓔ
10) Ⓐ Ⓑ Ⓒ Ⓓ Ⓔ   11) Ⓐ Ⓑ Ⓒ Ⓓ Ⓔ   12) Ⓐ Ⓑ Ⓒ Ⓓ Ⓔ
13) Ⓐ Ⓑ Ⓒ Ⓓ Ⓔ   14) Ⓐ Ⓑ Ⓒ Ⓓ Ⓔ   15) Ⓐ Ⓑ Ⓒ Ⓓ Ⓔ
16) Ⓐ Ⓑ Ⓒ Ⓓ Ⓔ   17) Ⓐ Ⓑ Ⓒ Ⓓ Ⓔ   18) Ⓐ Ⓑ Ⓒ Ⓓ Ⓔ
19) Ⓐ Ⓑ Ⓒ Ⓓ Ⓔ   20) Ⓐ Ⓑ Ⓒ Ⓓ Ⓔ   21) Ⓐ Ⓑ Ⓒ Ⓓ Ⓔ
22) Ⓐ Ⓑ Ⓒ Ⓓ Ⓔ   23) Ⓐ Ⓑ Ⓒ Ⓓ Ⓔ   24) Ⓐ Ⓑ Ⓒ Ⓓ Ⓔ
25) Ⓐ Ⓑ Ⓒ Ⓓ Ⓔ   26) Ⓐ Ⓑ Ⓒ Ⓓ Ⓔ   27) Ⓐ Ⓑ Ⓒ Ⓓ Ⓔ
28) Ⓐ Ⓑ Ⓒ Ⓓ Ⓔ   29) Ⓐ Ⓑ Ⓒ Ⓓ Ⓔ   30) Ⓐ Ⓑ Ⓒ Ⓓ Ⓔ
31) Ⓐ Ⓑ Ⓒ Ⓓ Ⓔ   32) Ⓐ Ⓑ Ⓒ Ⓓ Ⓔ   33) Ⓐ Ⓑ Ⓒ Ⓓ Ⓔ
34) Ⓐ Ⓑ Ⓒ Ⓓ Ⓔ   35) Ⓐ Ⓑ Ⓒ Ⓓ Ⓔ   36) Ⓐ Ⓑ Ⓒ Ⓓ Ⓔ
37) Ⓐ Ⓑ Ⓒ Ⓓ Ⓔ   38) Ⓐ Ⓑ Ⓒ Ⓓ Ⓔ   39) Ⓐ Ⓑ Ⓒ Ⓓ Ⓔ
40) Ⓐ Ⓑ Ⓒ Ⓓ Ⓔ   41) Ⓐ Ⓑ Ⓒ Ⓓ Ⓔ   42) Ⓐ Ⓑ Ⓒ Ⓓ Ⓔ
43) Ⓐ Ⓑ Ⓒ Ⓓ Ⓔ   44) Ⓐ Ⓑ Ⓒ Ⓓ Ⓔ   45) Ⓐ Ⓑ Ⓒ Ⓓ Ⓔ
46) Ⓐ Ⓑ Ⓒ Ⓓ Ⓔ   47) Ⓐ Ⓑ Ⓒ Ⓓ Ⓔ   48) Ⓐ Ⓑ Ⓒ Ⓓ Ⓔ
49) Ⓐ Ⓑ Ⓒ Ⓓ Ⓔ   50) Ⓐ Ⓑ Ⓒ Ⓓ Ⓔ

AFOQT Math Test 1
Arithmetic Reasoning

- **25 questions**
- **Total time for this section:** 29 Minutes
- **Calculators are not allowed at the test.**

AFOQT Math Practice Tests

1) Each year, a cyber café charges its customers a base rate of $12, with an additional $0.50 per visit for the first 50 visits, and $0.20 for every visit after that. How much does the cyber café charge a customer for a year in which 80 visits are made?

   (A) $43
   (B) $29
   (C) $38
   (D) $52

2) John is driving to visit his mother, who lives 200 miles away. How long will the drive be, round-trip, if John drives at an average speed of 50 mph?

   (A) 670 minutes
   (B) 540 minutes
   (C) 390 minutes
   (D) 600 minutes
   (E) 600 minutes
   (F) 600 minutes

3) If a vehicle is driven 20 miles on Monday, 30 miles on Tuesday, and 31 miles on Wednesday, what is the average number of miles driven each day?

   (A) 27 Miles
   (B) 18 Miles
   (C) 31 Miles
   (D) 25 Miles

4) Aria was hired to teach three identical math courses, which entailed being present in the classroom 27 hours altogether. At $36 per class hour, how much did Aria earn for teaching one course?

   (A) $1,200
   (B) $324
   (C) $200
   (D) $36
   (E) $36

5) Three co-workers contributed $13.25, $10.35, and $21.65 respectively to purchase a retirement gift for their boss. What is the maximum amount they can spend on a gift?

   (A) $37.15
   (B) $51.65
   (C) $45.25
   (D) $42.30

AFOQT Math Practice Tests

6) Karen is 12 years older than her sister Michelle, and Michelle is 3 years younger than her brother David. If the sum of their ages is 81, how old is Michelle?

   (A) 31
   (B) 25
   (C) 22
   (D) 18

7) You are asked to chart the temperature during an 8—hour period to give the average. These are your results:
   7 am: 2 degrees
   8 am: 5 degrees
   9 am: 22 degrees
   10 am: 28 degrees
   11 am: 32 degrees
   12 pm: 35 degrees
   1 pm: 35 degrees
   2 pm: 33 degrees
   What is the average temperature?

   (A) 36
   (B) 28
   (C) 24
   (D) 18

8) Julie gives 6 pieces of candy to each of her friends. If Julie gives all her candy away, which amount of candy could have been the amount she distributed?

   (A) 187
   (B) 216
   (C) 343
   (D) 223

9) If a rectangle is 25 feet by 30 feet, what is its area?

   (A) 750 feet^2
   (B) 480 feet^2
   (C) 290 feet^2
   (D) 800 feet^2

10) William is driving a truck that can hold 4 tons maximum. He has a shipment of food weighing 36,000 pounds. How many trips will he need to make to deliver all of the food?

    (A) 4 Trips
    (B) 6 Trips
    (C) 3 Trips
    (D) 5 Trips

AFOQT Math Practice Tests

11) A man goes to a casino with $150. He loses $50 on blackjack, then loses another $80 on roulette. How much money does he have left?

   (A) $28
   (B) $32
   (C) $20
   (D) $42

12) Will has been working on a report for 2 hours each day, 7 days a week for 3 weeks. How many minutes has will worked on his report?

   (A) 1,890 minutes
   (B) 3,780 minutes
   (C) 4,459 minutes
   (D) 2,520 minutes

13) In the deck of cards, there are 5 spades, 3 hearts, 8 clubs, and 10 diamonds. What is the probability that William will pick out a spade?

   (A) 1/14
   (B) 3/8
   (C) 2/13
   (D) 2/15

14) While at work, Emma checks her email once every 70 minutes. In 7−hour, how many times does she check her email?

   (A) 12 Times
   (B) 6 Times
   (C) 4 Times
   (D) 8 Times

15) A writer finishes 120 pages of his manuscript in 20 hours. How many pages is his average per hour?

   (A) 4
   (B) 18
   (C) 6
   (D) 12

AFOQT Math Practice Tests

16) A family owns 12 dozen of magazines. After donating 60 magazines to the public library, how many magazines are still with the family?

   (A) 84
   (B) 120
   (C) 76
   (D) 69

17) I've got 35 quarts of milk and my family drinks 5 gallons of milk per week. How many weeks will that last us?

   (A) 2.25 Weeks
   (B) 3.10 Weeks
   (C) 1.75 Weeks
   (D) 4.30 Weeks

18) What is the prime factorization of 336?

   (A) $2 \times 2 \times 5 \times 7$
   (B) $2 \times 2 \times 2 \times 2 \times 3 \times 7$
   (C) 2×7
   (D) $2 \times 2 \times 2 \times 5 \times 7$

19) A woman owns a dog walking business. If 4 workers can walk 8 dogs, how many dogs can 6 workers walk?

   (A) 12
   (B) 16
   (C) 14
   (D) 18

20) If one acre of forest contains 164 pine trees, how many pine trees are contained in 30 acres?

   (A) 4,920
   (B) 3,970
   (C) 5,170
   (D) 4,230

AFOQT Math Practice Tests

21) Five out of 25 students had to go to summer school. What is the ratio of students who did not have to go to summer school expressed, in its lowest terms?

   (A) $\frac{3}{5}$

   (B) $\frac{3}{7}$

   (C) $\frac{2}{3}$

   (D) $\frac{4}{5}$

22) A writer finishes 250 pages of his manuscript in 25 hours. How many pages is his average per hour?

   (A) 12

   (B) 5

   (C) 18

   (D) 10

23) Camille uses a 25% off coupon when buying a sweater that costs $50. If she also pays 4 sales tax on the purchase, how much does she pay?

   (A) $39

   (B) $44

   (C) $28

   (D) $32

24) Ava needs 1/5 of an ounce of salt to make 1 cup of dip for fries. How many cups of dip will she be able to make if she has 40 ounces of salt?

   (A) 14

   (B) 23

   (C) 30

   (D) 42

25) A floppy disk shows 937,025 bytes free and 740,350 bytes used. If you delete a file of size 650,160 bytes and create a new file of size 500,900 bytes, how many free bytes will the floppy disk have?

   (A) 1086,285

   (B) 956,285

   (C) 1060,270

   (D) 860,260

AFOQT Math Practice Test
Mathematics Knowledge

- **25 questions**
- **Total time for this section:** 22 Minutes
- **Calculators are not allowed at the test.**

26) If $-5a = 150$, then $a = $ ___

(A) -20
(B) -30
(C) 15
(D) 8

27) In the following right triangle, what is the value of x rounded to the nearest hundredth?

(A) 9.120
(B) 10.140
(C) 7.810
(D) 5.245

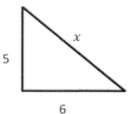

28) If $a = 2.5$, what is the value of b in this equation?
$b = \frac{a^2}{2} + 6$

(A) 10.75
(B) 15.20
(C) 20
(D) 12.25

29) A circle has a radius of 8 inches. What is its approximate area? ($\pi = 3.14$)

(A) 200.96 square inches
(B) 160.50 square inches
(C) 230.85 square inches
(D) 250.95 square inches

30) The eighth root of $6,561$ is:

(A) 2
(B) 4
(C) 3
(D) 5

31) In the following diagram what is the value of x?

(A) $60°$
(B) $90°$
(C) $15°$
(D) $45°$

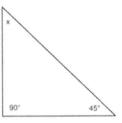

32) If $2^{12} = 2^7 \times 2^x$, what is the value of x?

(A) 5
(B) 10
(C) 2
(D) 8

33) Which of the following is an obtuse angle?

(A) $89°$
(B) $115°$
(C) $25°$
(D) $14°$

34) $(4x+2)(3x+8) =$?

(A) $12x^2 + 38x + 16$
(B) $12x^2 + 24x$
(C) $4x^2 - 10x + 8$
(D) $25x + 32$

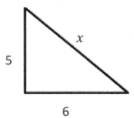

35) Find the slope of the line running through the points $(8,4)$ and $(5,2)$.

(A) $\frac{2}{3}$
(B) $\frac{4}{3}$
(C) $\frac{1}{8}$
(D) $\frac{2}{9}$

AFOQT Math Practice Tests

36) Which of the following is equal to 5^3?

   (A) the square of 5
   (B) 5 squared
   (C) 5 cubed
   (D) 5 to the second power

37) A square has one side with length 3.25 feet. The area of the square is:

   (A) 9 square feet
   (B) 10.56 square feet
   (C) 12.79 square feet
   (D) 18.43 square feet

38) $3(a - 9) = 22$, what is the value of a?

   (A) 12.90
   (B) 10
   (C) 15.24
   (D) 16.33

39) Factor this expression: $x^2 + 5 - 6$

   (A) $(x + 3)(x - 2)$
   (B) $(x + 6)(x - 1)$
   (C) $(x + 6)(x + 2)$
   (D) $(2x - 6)(x + 2)$

40) What's the area of the non-shaded part in the following figure?

   (A) 198
   (B) 120
   (C) 90
   (D) 78

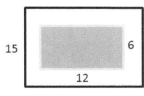

41) What's the square root of $25\ x^4$?

(A) $5\ x^2$
(B) $5\ \sqrt{x^2}$
(C) $2\ x^4$
(D) $5\ x^4$

42) A medium pizza has a diameter of 6 inches. What is its circumference?

(A) $9\ \pi$
(B) $4.5\ \pi$
(C) $6\ \pi$
(D) $12\ \pi$

43) The cube root of $2,744$ is?

(A) 18
(B) 21
(C) 15
(D) 14

44) What is the value of $\sqrt{169} \times \sqrt{25}$?

(A) 60
(B) 44
(C) 90
(D) 65

45) What is the circumference of a circle with center at point A if the distance from point X to Y is 30 feet? ($\pi = 3.14$)

(A) 94.2 feet
(B) 106.32 feet
(C) 59.56 feet
(D) 68.35 feet

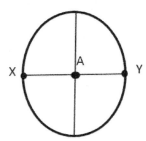

AFOQT Math Practice Tests

46) In the following diagram, the straight line is divided by one angled line at $115°$. What is the value of a?

   (A) $62°$
   (B) $65°$
   (C) $34°$
   (D) $58°$

47) What is $978,340$ in scientific notation?

   (A) 9.7834×10^5
   (B) 9.7834×10^3
   (C) 97.834×10^3
   (D) 97.834×10^6

48) If a circle has a diameter of 3.5 feet, what is its circumference?

   (A) 2.5π
   (B) 1.75π
   (C) 3.5π
   (D) 4π

49) A medium pizza has a diameter of 12 inches. What is its circumference?

   (A) 12π
   (B) 5π
   (C) 21π
   (D) 18π

50) Which of the following sets of factors do both 35 and 20 have in common?

   (A) $\{1, 2, 6\}$
   (B) $\{1, 4, 7\}$
   (C) $\{6, 13, 20\}$
   (D) $\{1, 2\}$

AFOQT Math Practice Test 2 Answer Sheet

Remove (or photocopy) this answer sheet and use it to complete the practice test

1) Ⓐ Ⓑ Ⓒ Ⓓ Ⓔ   2) Ⓐ Ⓑ Ⓒ Ⓓ Ⓔ   3) Ⓐ Ⓑ Ⓒ Ⓓ Ⓔ
4) Ⓐ Ⓑ Ⓒ Ⓓ Ⓔ   5) Ⓐ Ⓑ Ⓒ Ⓓ Ⓔ   6) Ⓐ Ⓑ Ⓒ Ⓓ Ⓔ
7) Ⓐ Ⓑ Ⓒ Ⓓ Ⓔ   8) Ⓐ Ⓑ Ⓒ Ⓓ Ⓔ   9) Ⓐ Ⓑ Ⓒ Ⓓ Ⓔ
10) Ⓐ Ⓑ Ⓒ Ⓓ Ⓔ   11) Ⓐ Ⓑ Ⓒ Ⓓ Ⓔ   12) Ⓐ Ⓑ Ⓒ Ⓓ Ⓔ
13) Ⓐ Ⓑ Ⓒ Ⓓ Ⓔ   14) Ⓐ Ⓑ Ⓒ Ⓓ Ⓔ   15) Ⓐ Ⓑ Ⓒ Ⓓ Ⓔ
16) Ⓐ Ⓑ Ⓒ Ⓓ Ⓔ   17) Ⓐ Ⓑ Ⓒ Ⓓ Ⓔ   18) Ⓐ Ⓑ Ⓒ Ⓓ Ⓔ
19) Ⓐ Ⓑ Ⓒ Ⓓ Ⓔ   20) Ⓐ Ⓑ Ⓒ Ⓓ Ⓔ   21) Ⓐ Ⓑ Ⓒ Ⓓ Ⓔ
22) Ⓐ Ⓑ Ⓒ Ⓓ Ⓔ   23) Ⓐ Ⓑ Ⓒ Ⓓ Ⓔ   24) Ⓐ Ⓑ Ⓒ Ⓓ Ⓔ
25) Ⓐ Ⓑ Ⓒ Ⓓ Ⓔ   26) Ⓐ Ⓑ Ⓒ Ⓓ Ⓔ   27) Ⓐ Ⓑ Ⓒ Ⓓ Ⓔ
28) Ⓐ Ⓑ Ⓒ Ⓓ Ⓔ   29) Ⓐ Ⓑ Ⓒ Ⓓ Ⓔ   30) Ⓐ Ⓑ Ⓒ Ⓓ Ⓔ
31) Ⓐ Ⓑ Ⓒ Ⓓ Ⓔ   32) Ⓐ Ⓑ Ⓒ Ⓓ Ⓔ   33) Ⓐ Ⓑ Ⓒ Ⓓ Ⓔ
34) Ⓐ Ⓑ Ⓒ Ⓓ Ⓔ   35) Ⓐ Ⓑ Ⓒ Ⓓ Ⓔ   36) Ⓐ Ⓑ Ⓒ Ⓓ Ⓔ
37) Ⓐ Ⓑ Ⓒ Ⓓ Ⓔ   38) Ⓐ Ⓑ Ⓒ Ⓓ Ⓔ   39) Ⓐ Ⓑ Ⓒ Ⓓ Ⓔ
40) Ⓐ Ⓑ Ⓒ Ⓓ Ⓔ   41) Ⓐ Ⓑ Ⓒ Ⓓ Ⓔ   42) Ⓐ Ⓑ Ⓒ Ⓓ Ⓔ
43) Ⓐ Ⓑ Ⓒ Ⓓ Ⓔ   44) Ⓐ Ⓑ Ⓒ Ⓓ Ⓔ   45) Ⓐ Ⓑ Ⓒ Ⓓ Ⓔ
46) Ⓐ Ⓑ Ⓒ Ⓓ Ⓔ   47) Ⓐ Ⓑ Ⓒ Ⓓ Ⓔ   48) Ⓐ Ⓑ Ⓒ Ⓓ Ⓔ
49) Ⓐ Ⓑ Ⓒ Ⓓ Ⓔ   50) Ⓐ Ⓑ Ⓒ Ⓓ Ⓔ

AFOQT Math Test 2
Arithmetic Reasoning

- **25 questions**
- **Total time for this section:** 29 Minutes
- **Calculators are not allowed at the test.**

AFOQT Math Practice Tests

1) You are asked to chart the temperature during a 5—hour period to give the average. These are your results:
   7 am: 10 degrees
   8 am: 12 degrees
   9 am: 25 degrees
   10 am: 28 degrees
   11 am: 28 degrees
   What is the average temperature?

   (A) 18.2

   (B) 31.8

   (C) 17.4

   (D) 20.6

2) Which of the following is NOT a factor of 40?

   (A) 10

   (B) 15

   (C) 20

   (D) 5

3) How many square feet of tile is needed for a 13 feet x 13 feet room?

   (A) 120 square feet

   (B) 70 square feet

   (C) 169 square feet

   (D) 214 square feet

4) In a classroom of 50 students, 32 are female. What percentage of the class is male?

   (A) 30%

   (B) 36%

   (C) 26%

   (D) 18%

5) Will has been working on a report for 4 hours each day, 7 days a week for 3 weeks. How many minutes has Will worked on his report?

   (A) 5,040 minutes

   (B) 84 minutes

   (C) 2,357 minutes

   (D) 42 minutes

6) With what number must 13.03317 be multiplied in order to obtain the number 1303.317?

   (A) 1,000
   (B) 10,000
   (C) 100
   (D) 10

7) During the last week of track training, Emma achieves the following times in seconds:
   66, 57, 54, 64, 57, and 59.
   Her three best times this week (least times) are averaged for her final score on the course. What is her final score?

   (A) 56 seconds
   (B) 32 seconds
   (C) 44 seconds
   (D) 69 seconds

8) James is driving to visit his mother, who lives 280 miles away. How long will the drive be, round-trip, if James drives at an average speed of 40 mph?

   (A) 84 minutes
   (B) 310 minutes
   (C) 840 minutes
   (D) 220 minutes

9) Emily and Lucas have taken the same number of photos on their school trip. Emily has taken 3 times as many photos as Mia. Lucas has taken 18 more photos than Mia. How many photos has Mia taken?

   (A) 9
   (B) 12
   (C) 7
   (D) 13

10) Find the average of the following numbers: 25, 31, 21, 18

    (A) 26
    (B) 23.75
    (C) 12
    (D) 32.24

AFOQT Math Practice Tests

11) The sum of 7 numbers is greater than 140 and less than 190. Which of the following could be the average (arithmetic mean) of the numbers?

   (A) 18
   (B) 26
   (C) 30
   (D) 34

12) A barista averages making 12 coffees per hour. At this rate, how many hours will it take until she's made 1,200 coffees?

   (A) 100 hours
   (B) 105 hours
   (C) 90 hours
   (D) 76 hours

13) Emma is working in a hospital supply room and makes $32.00 an hour. The union negotiates a new contract giving each employee a 2 cost of living raise. What is Emma's new hourly rate?

   (A) $25 an hour
   (B) $41 an hour
   (C) $32.64 an hour
   (D) $22.81 an hour

14) There are 150 rooms that need to be painted and only 15 painters available. If there are still 15 rooms unpainted by the end of the day, what is the average number of rooms that each painter has painted?

   (A) 7
   (B) 18
   (C) 14
   (D) 9

15) An architect's floor plan uses $\frac{1}{2}$ inch to represent one mile. What is the actual distance represented by $12 \frac{1}{2}$ inches?

   (A) 15 miles
   (B) 30 miles
   (C) 25 miles
   (D) 12 miles

AFOQT Math Practice Tests

16) Will has been working on a report for 7 hours each day, 5 days a week for 3 weeks. How many minutes has Will worked on his report?

   (A) 3,600 minutes

   (B) 2,645 minutes

   (C) 4,510 minutes

   (D) 4,200 minutes

17) A snack machine accepts only quarters. Candy bars cost 20¢, a package of peanuts costs 60¢, and a can of cola costs 45¢. How many quarters are needed to buy two Candy bars, one package of peanuts, and one can of cola?

   (A) 7 quarters

   (B) 5 quarters

   (C) 8 quarters

   (D) 6 quarters

18) A mobile classroom is a rectangular block that is 70 feet by 25 feet in length and width respectively. If a student walks around the block once, how many yards does the student cover?

   (A) 190 yards

   (B) 2,350 yards

   (C) 120 yards

   (D) 250 yards

19) What is the distance in miles of a trip that takes 2.1 hours at an average speed of 16.2 miles per hour? (Round your answer to a whole number)

   (A) 41 miles

   (B) 34 miles

   (C) 44 miles

   (D) 46 miles

20) What is the product of the square root of 169 and the square root of 81?

   (A) 117

   (B) 126

   (C) 98

   (D) 1,145

AFOQT Math Practice Tests

21) Nicole was making $5.50 per hour and got a raise to $6.75 per hour. What percentage increase was Nicole's raise?

   (A) 19.32%
   (B) 18.51%
   (C) 24.10%
   (D) 2.90%

22) A bread recipe calls for $4\frac{1}{6}$ cups of flour. If you only have $2\frac{1}{3}$ cups of flour, how much more flour is needed?

   (A) $-\frac{10}{7}$
   (B) $-\frac{5}{3}$
   (C) $-\frac{2}{7}$
   (D) $-\frac{1}{9}$

23) Convert 0.037 to a percent.

   (A) 37%
   (B) 3.7%
   (C) 0.37%
   (D) 0.037%

24) The hour hand of a watch rotates 25 degrees every hour. How many complete rotations does the hour hand make in 5 days?

   (A) 8
   (B) 16
   (C) 10
   (D) 12

25) If $3y + 2y + 5y = -30$, then what is the value of y?

   (A) -5
   (B) -3
   (C) -1
   (D) 0

AFOQT Math Practice Tests

AFOQT Math Practice Test
Mathematics Knowledge

- **25 questions**
- **Total time for this section:** 22 Minutes
- **Calculators are not allowed at the test.**

AFOQT Math Practice Tests

26) If x is a positive integer divisible by 6, and $x < 60$, what is the greatest possible value of x?

   (A) 54
   (B) 48
   (C) 36
   (D) 59

27) Which of the following is an obtuse angle?

   (A) $126°$
   (B) $85°$
   (C) $218°$
   (D) $64°$

28) $(x - 4)(x + 8) = ?$

   (A) $x^2 + 14x - 32$
   (B) $2x^2 + 14x - 41$
   (C) $x^2 + 4x - 32$
   (D) $x^2 + 3x + 18$

29) $7^3 \times 7^{10} = ?$

   (A) 7^{13}
   (B) 7^{30}
   (C) 7^7
   (D) 49^{30}

30) Convert $680,000$ to scientific notation.

   (A) 68×10^5
   (B) 6.8×10^3
   (C) 6.8×10^5
   (D) 6.8×10^7

31) A circle has a diameter of 12 inches. What is its approximate area? ($\pi = 3.14$)

   (A) 120.64 in^2
   (B) 100.25 in^2
   (C) 113.04 in^2
   (D) 95.24 in^2

32) What is the perimeter of the triangle in the provided diagram?

   (A) 34
   (B) 72
   (C) 60
   (D) 25

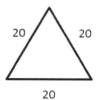

33) The cube root of 343 is?

   (A) 7
   (B) 6
   (C) 12
   (D) 9

34) Which of the following is the correct calculation for $5!$?

   (A) $6 \times 5 \times 4 \times 3 \times 2 \times 1$
   (B) $1 \times 2 \times 3 \times 4 \times 5 \times 6 \times 7$
   (C) $5 \times 4 \times 3 \times 2 \times 1$
   (D) $5 \times 4 \times 3 \times 2 \times 1 \times 0$

35) $x^2 - 49 = 0$, x could be:

   (A) 7
   (B) 10
   (C) 9
   (D) 6

AFOQT Math Practice Tests

36) There are two pizza ovens in a restaurant. Oven 1 burns four times as many pizzas as oven 2. If the restaurant had a total of 15 burnt pizzas on Saturday, how many pizzas did oven 2 burn?

   (A) 3
   (B) 9
   (C) 6
   (D) 12

37) A rectangular plot of land is measured to be 120 feet by 180 feet. Its total area is:

   (A) 32,450 square feet
   (B) 8,850 square feet
   (C) 21,600 square feet
   (D) 18,920 square feet

38) What is 6731.38236 rounded to the nearest tenth?

   (A) 6731.3
   (B) 6731.5
   (C) 6731.4
   (D) 6731.39

39) What is the distance between the points $(1, 5)$ and $(-1, 9)$?

   (A) $3\sqrt{3}$
   (B) $3\sqrt{2}$
   (C) $2\sqrt{3}$
   (D) $2\sqrt{2}$

40) The equation of a line is given as: $y = 2x - 5$. Which of the following points lie on the line?

   (A) $(1, 2)$
   (B) $(-2, -9)$
   (C) $(3, 18)$
   (D) $(2, 7)$

AFOQT Math Practice Tests

41) With what number must 6.123459 be multiplied in order to obtain the number $61,234.59$?

   (A) $10,000$
   (B) $1,000$
   (C) 100
   (D) 10

42) The sum of 5 numbers is greater than 340 and less than 400. Which of the following could be the average (arithmetic mean) of the numbers?

   (A) 80
   (B) 70
   (C) 60
   (D) 90

43) How long is the line segment shown on the number line below?

   (A) 7
   (B) -7
   (C) -9
   (D) 9

44) What is the sum of the prime numbers in the following list of numbers?
    $14, 12, 11, 16, 13, 20, 19, 36, 30$

   (A) 48
   (B) 37
   (C) 43
   (D) 25

45) Which of the following is NOT a factor of 60?

   (A) 10
   (B) 30
   (C) 5
   (D) 8

46) The supplement angle of a $51°$ angle is:

   (A) $148°$
   (B) $87°$
   (C) $39°$
   (D) $129°$

47) Simplify: $4(3x^5)^2$.

   (A) $30x^{12}$
   (B) $25x^4$
   (C) $36x^{10}$
   (D) $26x^8$

48) One third the cube of 3 is:

   (A) 9
   (B) 12
   (C) 7
   (D) 6

49) 25% of 70 is:

   (A) 12.6
   (B) 27
   (C) 35
   (D) 17.5

50) Convert 32% to a fraction.

   (A) $\frac{8}{19}$
   (B) $\frac{8}{25}$
   (C) $\frac{3}{17}$
   (D) $\frac{2}{21}$

AFOQT Mathematics Practice Test

Mathematical Reasoning Practice Test
Answers and Explanations

AFOQT Practice Test 1

1)	A	2)	D	3)	A
4)	B	5)	C	6)	C
7)	C	8)	B	9)	A
10)	D	11)	C	12)	D
13)	C	14)	B	15)	C
16)	A	17)	C	18)	B
19)	A	20)	A	21)	D
22)	D	23)	A	24)	C
25)	A	26)	B	27)	C
28)	D	29)	A	30)	C
31)	D	32)	A	33)	B
34)	A	35)	B	36)	C
37)	B	38)	D	39)	B
40)	A	41)	A	42)	C
43)	D	44)	D	45)	A
46)	B	47)	A	48)	C
49)	A	50)	D		

AFOQT Practice Test 2

1)	D	2)	B	3)	C
4)	B	5)	A	6)	C
7)	A	8)	C	9)	A
10)	B	11)	B	12)	A
13)	C	14)	D	15)	C
16)	D	17)	B	18)	A
19)	C	20)	A	21)	B
22)	B	23)	B	24)	C
25)	B	26)	A	27)	A
28)	C	29)	A	30)	C
31)	C	32)	C	33)	A
34)	C	35)	A	36)	A
37)	C	38)	C	39)	C
40)	B	41)	A	42)	B
43)	D	44)	C	45)	D
46)	D	47)	C	48)	A
49)	D	50)	B		

AFOQT Math Practice Tests Explanations

In this section, answers and explanations are provided for the AFOQT Practice Math Tests. Review the answers and explanations to learn more about solving AFOQT Math questions fast.

AFOQT Math Practice Test 1
Answers and Explanations

1) Choice A is correct
The base rate is $12.
The fee for the first 50 visits is: $50 \times 0.50 = 25$
The fee for the visits 51 to 80 is: $30 \times 0.20 = 6$
Total charge: $12 + 25 + 6 = 43$

2) Choice D is correct
distance = speed × time ⇒ time = $\frac{distance}{speed} = \frac{500}{50} = 10$
(Round trip means that the distance is 500 miles)
The round trip takes 10 hours.
Change hours to minutes, then: $10 \times 60 = 600$

3) Choice A is correct
average = $\frac{sum}{total}$
average = $\frac{20 + 30 + 31}{3} = \frac{81}{3} = 27$

4) Choice B is correct
$27 \div 3 = 9$ hours for one course
$9 \times 36 = 324 \Rightarrow \$324$

5) Choice C is correct
The amount they have = $\$13.25 + \$10.35 + \$21.65 = \$45.25$

6) Choice C is correct
Michelle = Karen − 12
Michelle = David − 3
Karen + Michelle + David = 81
Now, replace the ages of Karen and David by Michelle. Then:
Michelle + 12 + Michelle + Michelle + 3 = 81
3 Michelle + 15 = 81 ⇒ 3 Michelle = 81 − 15
3 Michelle = 66
Michelle = 22

AFOQT Math Practice Tests

7) Choice C is correct
average $= \frac{sum}{total}$
Sum $= 2 + 5 + 22 + 28 + 32 + 35 + 35 + 33 = 192$
Total number of numbers $= 8$
average $= \frac{192}{8} = 24$

8) Choice B is correct
Since Julie gives 6 pieces of candy to each of her friends, then, then number of pieces of candies must be divisible by 6.
A. $187 \div 6 = 31.166$
B. $216 \div 6 = 36$
C. $343 \div 6 = 57.166$
D. $223 \div 6 = 37.166$
Only choice B gives a whole number.

9) Choice A is correct
Area of a rectangle $=$ width $\times$ length $= 25 \times 30 = 750$

10) Choice D is correct
1 ton $= 2,000$ pounds
4 ton $= 8,000$ pounds
$\frac{36,000}{8,000} = 4.5$
William needs to make at least 5 trips to deliver all of the food.

11) Choice C is correct
$150 - 50 - 80 = 20$

12) Choice D is correct
3 weeks $= 21$ days
$21 \times 2 = 42$ hours
$42 \times 60 = 2,520$ minutes

13) Choice C is correct
probability $= \frac{desired\ outcomes}{possible\ outcomes} = \frac{4}{5+3+8+10} = \frac{4}{26} = \frac{2}{13}$

14) Choice B is correct
Change 7 hours to minutes, then: $7 \times 60 = 420$ minutes
$\frac{420}{70} = 6$

AFOQT Math Practice Tests

15) Choice C is correct
$\frac{120}{20} = 6$

16) Choice A is correct
12 dozen of magazines are 144 magazines: $12 \times 12 = 144$
$144 - 60 = 84$

17) Choice C is correct
1 quart $= 0.25$ gallon
35 quarts $= 35 \times 0.25 = 8.75$ gallons
then: $\frac{8.75}{5} = 1.75$ weeks

18) Choice B is correct
Find the value of each choice:
A. $2 \times 2 \times 5 \times 7 = 140$
B. $2 \times 2 \times 2 \times 2 \times 3 \times 7 = 336$
C. $2 \times 7 = 14$
D. $2 \times 2 \times 2 \times 5 \times 7 = 280$

19) Choice A is correct
Each worker can walk 2 dogs: $8 \div 4 = 2$
6 workers can walk 12 dogs.
$6 \times 2 = 12$

20) Choice A is correct
Write proportion and solve. $\frac{1}{164} = \frac{30}{x} \Rightarrow x = 30 \times 164 = 4,920$

21) Choice D is correct
20 students did not have to go to summer school.
$25 - 5 = 20$
$\frac{20}{25} = \frac{4}{5}$

22) Choice D is correct
average $= \frac{sum}{total} = \frac{250}{25} = 10$

23) Choice A is correct
$25\% \times 50 = \frac{25}{100} \times 50 = 12.5$
The coupon has $12.5 value.
Then, the selling price of the sweater is $37.5.
$50 - 12.5 = 37.5$, Add 4% tax, then: $\frac{4}{100} \times 37.5 = 1.5$ for tax, Total: $37.5 + 1.5 = \$39$

AFOQT Math Practice Tests

24) Choice C is correct
Write a proportion and solve.
$\frac{1/5}{1} = \frac{45}{x} \implies x = \frac{45}{1/5} = 30$

25) Choice A is correct
The difference of the file added, and the file deleted is:
$650,160 - 500,900 = 149,260$
$937,025 + 149,260 = 1086,285$

26) Choice B is correct
$-5a = 150 \Rightarrow a = \frac{150}{-5} = -30$

27) Choice C is correct
Use Pythagorean Theorem: $a^2 + b^2 = c^2$
$(5)^2 + (6)^2 = c^2 \Rightarrow$
$25 + 36 = 61 = C^2$
$C = \sqrt{61} = 7.810$

28) Choice D is correct
If $a = 2.5$ then:
$b = \frac{a^2}{2} + 6 \Rightarrow b = \frac{2.5^2}{2} + 6 = 6.25 + 6 = 12.25$

29) Choice A is correct
(r = radius)
Area of a circle $= \pi r^2 = \pi \times (8)^2 = 3.14 \times 64 = 200.96$

30) Choice C is correct
$\sqrt[8]{6,561} = 3$
$3^8 = 3 \times 3 \times 3 \times 3 \times 3 \times 3 \times 3 \times 3 \times = 6,561$

31) Choice D is correct
All angles in a triable add up to 180 degrees.
$90° + 45° = 135°$
$x = 180° - 135° = 45°$

32) Choice A is correct
Use exponent multiplication rule:
$x^a \cdot x^b = x^{a+b}$
Then: $2^{12} = 2^7 \times 2^x = 2^{7+x} \Rightarrow$
$x = 12 - 7 = 5$

AFOQT Math Practice Tests

33) Choice B is correct
An obtuse angle is an angle of greater than 90 degrees and less than 180 degrees.
Only choice B is an obtuse angle.

34) Choice A is correct
Use FOIL (first, out, in, last) method.
$(4x + 2)(3x + 8) = 12x^2 + 32x + 6x + 16 = 12x^2 + 38x + 16$

35) Choice B is correct
Slope of a line: $\frac{y_2 - y_1}{x_2 - x1} = \frac{rise}{run}$
$\frac{y_2 - y_1}{x_2 - x1} = \frac{3 - 7}{5 - 8} = \frac{-4}{-3} = \frac{4}{3}$

36) Choice C is correct

37) Choice B is correct
Area of a square = (one side)^2 ⇒
A = $(3.25)^2$ ⇒
A = 10.56

38) Choice D is correct
$3(a - 9) = 22 \Rightarrow$
$3a - 27 = 22 \Rightarrow$
$3a = 27 + 22 = 49 \Rightarrow$
$3a = 49 \Rightarrow$
$a = \frac{49}{3} = 16.33$

39) Choice B is correct
To factor the expression $x^2 + 5 - 6$, we need to find two numbers whose sum is 5 and their product is -6.
Those numbers are 6 and -1.
Then: $x^2 + 5 - 6 = (x + 6)(x - 1)$

40) Choice A is correct
The area of the non-shaded region is equal to the area of the bigger rectangle subtracted by the area of smaller rectangle.
Area of the bigger rectangle = 15 × 18 = 270
Area of the smaller rectangle = 12 × 6 = 72
Area of the non-shaded region = 270 − 72 = 198

AFOQT Math Practice Tests

41) Choice A is correct
$\sqrt{25\,x^4} = \sqrt{25}\,\sqrt{x^4} = 5 \times x^2 = 5\,x^2$

42) Choice C is correct
Diameter $= 2\,r \Rightarrow 6 = 2\,r \Rightarrow r = 3$
Circumference $= 2\,\pi\,r \Rightarrow C = 2\,\pi\,(3) \Rightarrow C = 6\,\pi$

43) Choice D is correct
$\sqrt[3]{2,744} = 14$

44) Choice D is correct
$\sqrt{169} = 13,\ \sqrt{25} = 5$
$13 \times 5 = 65$

45) Choice A is correct
Diameter $= 2\,r \Rightarrow 30 = 2\,r \Rightarrow r = 15$
Circumference $= 2\,\pi\,r \Rightarrow C = 2\,\pi\,(15) \Rightarrow C = 30 \times 3.14 = 94.2$

46) Choice B is correct
The straight line is **180** degrees. Then:
a $= 180° - 115° = 65°$

47) Choice A is correct
In scientific notation form, numbers are written with one whole number times **10** to the power of a whole number. Number **978,340** has **6** digits. Write the number and after the first digit put the decimal point.
Then, multiply the number by **10** to the power of **5** (number of remaining digits). Then:
$978,340 = 9.7834 \times 10^5$

48) Choice C is correct
Diameter $= 2\,r \Rightarrow 3.5 = 2\,r \Rightarrow r = 1.75$
Circumference $= 2\,\pi\,r \Rightarrow C = 2\,\pi\,(1.75) \Rightarrow C = 3.5\,\pi$

49) Choice A is correct
Diameter $= 2\,r \Rightarrow 12 = 2\,r \Rightarrow r = 6$
Circumference $= 2\,\pi\,r \Rightarrow C = 2\,\pi\,(6) \Rightarrow C = 12\,\pi$

50) Choice D is correct
Factor of **78** : $\{1, 2, 3, 6, 13, 26, 39\}$
Factor of **20** : $\{1, 2, 4, 5, 10, 20\}$
Then, factors they have in common is $\{1, 2\}$

AFOQT Math Practice Tests Explanations

In this section, answers and explanations are provided for the AFOQT Practice Math Tests. Review the answers and explanations to learn more about solving AFOQT Math questions fast.

AFOQT Math Practice Test 2
Answers and Explanations

1) Choice D is correct
average = $\frac{sum}{total}$
Sum = $10 + 12 + 25 + 28 + 28 = 103$
Total number of numbers = 5
$\frac{103}{5} = 20.6$

2) Choice B is correct
The factors of 40 are:
$\{1, 2, 4, 5, 8, 10, 20, 40\}$
15 is not a factor of 40.

3) Choice C is correct
The area of a 13 feet x 13 feet room is 169 square feet.
$13 \times 13 = 169$

4) Choice B is correct
$50 - 32 = 18$ male students
$\frac{18}{60} = 0.6$
Change 0.36 to percent $\Rightarrow 0.36 \times 100 = 36\%$

5) Choice A is correct
3 weeks = 21 days
Then: $21 \times 4 = 84$ hours
$84 \times 60 = 5,040$ minutes

6) Choice C is correct
$13.03317 \times 100 = 1303.317$

AFOQT Math Practice Tests

7) Choice A is correct
Emma's three best times are 54, 57, and 57.
The average of these numbers is:
average $= \frac{sum}{total}$
Sum $= 54 + 57 + 57 = 168$
Total number of numbers $= 3$
average $= \frac{168}{3} = 56$

8) Choice C is correct
distance $=$ speed $\times$ time $\Rightarrow$
time $= \frac{distance}{speed} = \frac{280 + 280}{40} = 14$
(Round trip means that the distance is 560 miles)
The round trip takes 14 hours.
Change hours to minutes, then: $14 \times 60 = 840$

9) Choice A is correct
Emily $=$ Lucas
Emily $= 3$ Mia $\Rightarrow$ Lucas $= 3$ Mia
Lucas $=$ Mia $+ 18$
then: Lucas $=$ Mia $+ 18 \Rightarrow 3$ Mia $=$ Mia $+ 18$
Remove 1 Mia from both sides of the equation. Then:
2 Mia $= 18 \Rightarrow$ Mia $= 9$

10) Choice B is correct
Sum $= 25 + 31 + 21 + 18 = 95$
average $= \frac{95}{4} = 23.75$

11) Choice B is correct
Let's review the choices provided and find their sum.
A. $18 \times 7 = 126$
B. $26 \times 7 = 182 \Rightarrow$ is greater than 140 and less than 190
C. $30 \times 7 = 210$
D. $34 \times 7 = 238$
Only choice b gives a number that is greater than 140 and less than 190.

12) Choice A is correct
$\frac{1\ hour}{12\ coffees} = \frac{x}{1200} \Rightarrow$
$12 \times x = 1 \times 1,200 \Rightarrow$
$12\ x1,200 = 100$
It takes 100 hours until she's made 1,200 coffees.

AFOQT Math Practice Tests

13)
Choice C is correct
2 percent of 32 is: $32 \times \frac{2}{100} = 0.64$
Emma's new rate is 32.64.
$32 + 0.64 = 32.64$

14)
Choice D is correct
$150 - 15 = 135$
$\frac{135}{15} = 9$

15)
Choice C is correct
Write a proportion and solve.
$\frac{\frac{1}{2} \, inches}{12.5} = \frac{1 \, miles}{x}$
Use cross multiplication, then: $12.5 \, x = 0.5 \rightarrow x = 25$

16)
Choice D is correct
10 days, $10 \times 7 = 70$ hours, $70 \times 60 = 4,200$ minutes

17)
Choice B is correct
Two candy bars costs 20¢ and a package of peanuts cost 60¢ and a can of cola costs 45¢.
The total cost is: $20 + 60 + 45 = 125$
125 is equal to 5 quarters.
$5 \times 25 = 125$

18)
Choice A is correct
Perimeter of a rectangle $= 2 \times$ length $+ 2 \times$ width $=$
$2 \times 70 + 2 \times 25 = 140 + 50 = 190$

19)
Choice C is correct
speed $= \frac{distance}{time}$
$18.4 = \frac{distance}{2.4} \Rightarrow$
distance $= 18.4 \times 2.4 = 44.16$
Rounded to a whole number, the answer is 44.

AFOQT Math Practice Tests

20) Choice A is correct
$\sqrt{169} \times \sqrt{81} = 13 \times 9 = 117$

21) Choice B is correct
percent of change $= \frac{change}{original\ number}$
$6.75 - 5.50 = 1.25$
percent of change $= \frac{1.25}{6.75} = 0.1851 \Rightarrow$
$0.1851 \times 100 = 18.51\%$

22) Choice B is correct
$4\frac{1}{6} - 2\frac{1}{3} = 4\frac{1}{6} - 2\frac{2}{6} = \frac{4}{6} - \frac{14}{6} = \frac{4-14}{6} = -\frac{10}{6} = -\frac{5}{3}$

23) Choice B is correct
To convert a decimal to percent, multiply it by 100 and then add percent sign (%).
$0.037 \times 100 = 3.7\%$

24) Choice C is correct
Every day the hour hand of a watch makes 2 complete rotation.
Thus, it makes 10 complete rotations in 5 days.
$2 \times 5 = 10$

25) Choice B is correct
$3y + 2y + 5y = -30 \Rightarrow$
$10y = -30 \Rightarrow y = -\frac{30}{10} \Rightarrow y = -3$

26) Choice A is correct
From the choices provided, 36, 48 and 54 are divisible by 6.
From these numbers, 54 is the biggest.

27) Choice A is correct
An obtuse angle is an angle of greater than $90°$ and less than $180°$.

28) Choice C is correct
Use FOIL (First, Out, In, Last) method.
$(x-4)(x+8) = x^2 + 8x - 4x - 32 = x^2 + 4x - 32$

AFOQT Math Practice Tests

29) Choice A is correct
Use exponent multiplication rule:
$x^a \cdot x^b = x^{a+b}$
$7^3 \times 7^{10} = 7^{13}$

30) Choice C is correct
In scientific notation form, numbers are written with one whole number times 10 to the power of a whole number.
Number $680,000$ has 6 digits.
Write the number and after the first digit put the decimal point. Then, multiply the number by 10 to the power of 5
(number of remaining digits).
Then: $680,000 = 6.8 \times 10^5$

31) Choice C is correct
Diameter $= 12$
then: Radius $= 6$
Area of a circle $= \pi r^2 \Rightarrow$
A $= 3.14 \, (6)^2 = 113.04$

32) Choice C is correct
Perimeter of a triangle $= side_1 + side_2 + side_3 = 20 + 20 + 20 = 60$

33) Choice A is correct
$\sqrt[3]{343} = 7$

34) Choice C is correct

35) Choice A is correct
$x^2 - 49 = 0 \Rightarrow$
$x^2 = 49 \Rightarrow x$ could be 7 or -7.

36) Choice A is correct
Oven 1 $=$ 4 oven 2
If Oven 2 burns 3 then oven 1 burns 12 pizzas.
$3 + 12 = 15$

AFOQT Math Practice Tests

37) Choice C is correct
Area of a rectangle = width × length = $120 \times 180 = 21,600$ square feet

38) Choice C is correct
6731.38236 rounded to the nearest tenth equals 6731.4
(Because 7631.38 is closer to $6,731.4$ than $6,731.3$)

39) Choice C is correct
Use distance formula:
$d = \sqrt{(x_1 - x_2)^2 + (y_1 - y_2)^2} =$
$\sqrt{(1-(-1))^2 + (5-9)^2}$
$\sqrt{4+8} = \sqrt{12} = 2\sqrt{3}$

40) Choice B is correct
Let's review the choices provided.
Put the values of x and y in the equation.
A. $(1, 2) \Rightarrow x = 1 \Rightarrow y = 2$ This is not true!
B. $(-2, -9) \Rightarrow x = -2 \Rightarrow y = -13$ This is true!
C. $(3, 18) \Rightarrow x = 3 \Rightarrow y = 12$ This is not true!
D. $(2, 7) \Rightarrow x = 2 \Rightarrow y = 7$ This is not true!

41) Choice A is correct
Number 6.123459 should be multiplied by $10,000$ in order to obtain the number $61,234.59$
$6.123459 \times 10,000 = 61,234.59$

42) Choice B is correct
Let's review the choices provided.
A. $70 \times 5 = 350$
B. $85 \times 5 = 425$
C. $90 \times 5 = 450$
D. $95 \times 5 = 475$
From choices provided, only 350 is greater than 340 and less than 400.

43) Choice D is correct
$1 - (-8) = 1 + 8 = 9$

44) Choice C is correct
From the list of numbers, 11, 13, and 19 are prime numbers.
Their sum is:
$11 + 13 + 19 = 43$

45) Choice D is correct
factor of $60 = \{1, 2, 4, 5, 6, 10, 12, 15, 30, 60\}$
8 is not a factor of 60.

46) Choice D is correct
Two Angles are supplementary when they add up to 180 degrees.
$129° + 51° = 180°$

47) Choice C is correct
$4(3x^5)^2 \Rightarrow 4 \times 3^2 \times x^{10} = 36\, x^{10}$

48) Choice A is correct
The cube of $3 = 3 \times 3 \times 3 = 27$
$\frac{1}{3} \times 27 = 9$

49) Choice D is correct
$\frac{25}{100} \times 70 = 17.5$

50) Choice B is correct
$32\% = \frac{32}{100} = \frac{8}{25}$

Receive the PDF version of this book or get another FREE book!

Thank you for using our Book!

Do you LOVE this book?

Then, you can get the PDF version of this book or another book absolutely FREE!

Please email us at:

info@Testinar.com

for details.

Made in the USA
Middletown, DE
27 June 2025

77598886R00124